BARDO

INTERVAL OF POSSIBILITY

BARDO

INTERVAL OF POSSIBILITY

Khenpo Karthar Rinpoche's
Commentary on *Aspiration for the Bardo*
by Chökyi Wangchuk

Translated by Yeshe Gyamtso

KTD Publications
Woodstock, New York

Published by:
KTD Publications
335 Meads Mountain Road
Woodstock, NY 12498, USA
www.KTDPublications.org

Distributed by:
Namse Bangdzo Bookstore
335 Meads Mountain Road
Woodstock, NY 12498, USA
www.NamseBangdzo.com

ISBN 0-9741092-2-3
This book is printed on acid free recycled paper

CONTENTS

INTRODUCTION

This book is the finished outcome of a teaching on dying, death, and the bardo given by Khenpo Karthar Rinpoche at the KTC (Karma Thegsum Chöling) center in Hartford, Connecticut on June 4th-6th, 2004. Khenpo Rinpoche gives a traditional presentation in the form of an extensive oral commentary on the brief root text, *Aspiration for the Bardo* (Tib. bar do'i smon lam), by Chökyi Wangchuk, the Sixth Shamarpa, found in the communal liturgy *Dharma Practices of the Karma Kagyu* (Tib. kam tshang chos spyod).

Chökyi Wangchuk, the Sixth Shamar Rinpoche (1584-c.1635), was recognized at an early age by his principal guru, the Ninth Gyalwang Karmapa, Wangchuk Dorje. Demonstrating swift accomplishment in his training and tremendous proficiency in debate and scholarship, he became one of the most renowned panditas of his era. He traveled and taught extensively throughout Tibet, China, and Nepal, and performed vast activity for the benefit of beings. Just as the Golden Garland of the Kagyu succession continued with Chökyi Wangchuk himself, he in turn recognized the tenth incarnation of the Gyalwang Karmapa, Chöying Dorje, who then became his principal disciple.

By far, the most widely known cycle of teachings dealing with the interval (Tib. bar do) is the *Great Liberation Through Hearing in the Bardo* (Tib. bar do thos drol chen mo), or, as it is commonly referred to in the West, the *Tibetan Book of the Dead.* A treasure text composed in the eighth century by Padmasambhava of Oddiyana, and later discovered in the fourteenth century by the great treasure revealer Karma Lingpa, it is an extraordinary compendium of precise and detailed knowledge and instruction pertaining to the bardo—the intermediate states of existence between life and death. Taken as a whole, however, the scope of the work is far too vast to be adequately encompassed by a teaching event of only three days' time.

Because of this, Khenpo Karthar Rinpoche thus explains that the reason why he chose Chökyi Wangchuk's *Aspiration for the Bardo* as the root text for his teaching and commentary is that although this aspiration liturgy is composed in brief verse form, it is nonetheless complete in its content and presentation. It is an appropriate and aptly-chosen work for the scope of a concise teaching such as this, and Khenpo Rinpoche bestows an exceptionally clear and accessible elucidation of this most challenging material, while graciously giving the necessary time and attention to its more technically obscure points.

His commentary is not merely a bare description of the sequence of events in the process of dying and death, but moreover, it is underscored throughout with the purpose and urgency of aspiration: we are clearly instructed on what to practice and how to train ourselves at every point of opportunity, in this very life—whether in the waking state or the dream state—and even within the interval experience itself, and we are exhorted to do so. Much of the basis of this preparation for the time of death hinges on a critical experiential understanding of the illusory nature of all appearances that is primarily obtained through meditation. Likewise, this understanding is closely interrelated with the gradual process of familiarization with the clear light—the very nature of mind itself. It is such familiarization through experience that will ultimately culminate in direct recognition of that nature, and as Khenpo Karthar Rinpoche explains, this is precisely what transforms the potential terror and confusion of the bardo into one of the greatest opportunities one could ever have—the interval of possibility.

It is a rare and invaluable blessing indeed to come into contact with these profound teachings. Rather than live our lives in anxiety, fear, and denial of death's inevitability, we can instead take confidence and joyfully look forward to making this life meaningful in preparing now for the tremendous opportunity for liberation that the time of death provides.

Jigme Nyima

This book is dedicated to
Khenpo Karthar Rinpoche,
our glorious guru of infinite unwavering
generosity, wisdom, and compassion.

THE BARDO

The best known explanation of the bardo is the *Great Liberation Through Hearing in the Bardo*, which provides a complete and precise explanation of what happens in the bardo as well as what you can do to deal with it and what opportunities there are for liberation. Because of the book's length and the relatively short space available here, the text that I use as the basis for this presentation is an aspiration liturgy called the *Aspiration for the Bardo*, which is also a complete treatment of the subject.

SUPPLICATING THE GURU

"Those who are our refuge in this life, in future lives, and in the interval in between, our guides, the gurus, I supplicate you. Lead us, who through negative karma mistake the projections of our bewilderment to be real, out of our wandering through the six states within samsara." The liturgy of aspiration begins with this supplication.

The first point is that our gurus are our sources of refuge, not only in this life and in all future lives, but also in the intervals or bardos in between lives. In this case, your gurus are those who hold you and raise you onto the path, such as the Golden Garland of the Kagyu. You begin by supplicating them expressly and by implication the other sources of refuge: the Buddha, Dharma, and Sangha.

The request you make in supplicating them is explained in the second sentence, which points out that it is through accruing negative karma that we wander in samsara. Your accumulation of negative karma is caused by mistaking your own bewildered projections or appearances to be real. That is to say that the appearances that you experience are functions of your bewilderment and are not independent realities. It is through mistaking them to be independently existent or independently real that you become fixated, generate kleshas, and accumulate negative karma. It is this that causes us to wander through and be reborn in the six states—the realms of the hells, pretas, animals, humans, asuras, and devas. Supplicating that you be led out of this introduces the whole aspiration, which is concerned with the discovery of the nature of bewildered appearances. You will see, as the liturgy goes through the various aspects of the bardo, that it is concerned with the penetration of appearances and the discovery of their true nature.

We begin with a definition of the bardo as we usually use the term. The term interval or bardo simply means "something that is in between two other things." It can be used and explained in different ways, but generally speaking it means the type of existence that you have in between lives when you have not gone to or reached the next state of birth. Here we use the term bardo to mean just that, and what characterizes it is explained in the next line, "In that state, one has no freedom or control."

For reasons that will become clear, beings in the bardo, being driven about by the strong force of karma, have no ability to control where they go. Your previous actions control you in the bardo, and you are driven by this karma. This means that you are thrown violently from one place to another without having the ability to stop. Now, if that is what the bardo is like, what can you do about it? That is explained, "Through the instructions concerning special visualizations for use at that time, may I be able to practice all the various ways of bringing the bardo to the path."

Because in the bardo state you have no opportunity to engage in practices, you must practice in the preceding life in order to gain control over the bardo. First you aspire to recognize what the bardo experience is. Then your aspiration is to be motivated by that recognition to pursue the practices that will give you the ability to gain control, and ideally liberation, within the bardo. Whereas before we used the term *bardo* in the restricted sense, to refer merely to the period in between lives, it will now be used in other senses as well, with practices consisting of specific methods, types of focus, or visualizations. All of these are ways to bring various aspects or stages of the bardo experience onto the path. That is what you refer to when you say, "May I undertake the specific practices that will bring the bardo onto the path."

The bardo basically has three phases, and the methods taught for dealing with these involve learning to see the particular type of bewildered projection that characterizes each phase. You recognize dharmata in the case of the first phase, deity and mantra in the case of the second, and the nirmanakaya or emanation body in the case of the third. These will be described in detail later on.

Nature and Aspects

The text now describes the true nature of the bardo, "If you examine it, you will see that there is no beginning or end, and therefore there can be no in-between." "It" here refers to the beginningless and potentially endless cycle of samsaric existence. If you examine existence, you will see that it is without beginning. Furthermore if you examine any phenomenon, you will see that it has no true arising. Because existence has no beginning, and because that which does not truly arise does not truly cease, there is therefore no abiding state that is in between. Ultimately speaking, there is no single state that is in between two other states because none of these other states have ever truly arisen or truly occurred. Therefore, in the context of absolute truth, what we call the "bardo" does not exist, but it certainly seems to exist to the person who is experiencing it. "Nevertheless in the context of bewilderment, it arises as a mere interdependent appearance."

The phrase "in the context of bewilderment" means

experience as you know it. Your experiencing cognition is obscured and therefore bewildered, and you therefore take things that do not have true or independent existence to have such existence. The appearance of the bardo is itself interdependent. It is the mere appearance of interdependent conditions, and in your bewilderment you mistake interdependent appearances to be independent and the bardo to be an independent reality. In other words, although the bardo does not really exist, it seems to exist as long as you are bewildered. No phenomenon ever truly arises, and thus any phenomenon that we can isolate is a mere interdependent appearance. That which never truly came into existence cannot go out of existence, so we can say that the phenomenon never truly ceases. Furthermore, the phenomenon cannot truly abide or persist in between origination and cessation, since it is empty of true origination. Although you may agree with that, you also have to admit that you experience the appearance of origination of phenomena. The phenomena seem to start to exist; you seem to experience their ending, destruction, or cessation as well as their abiding. The origination, cessation, and abiding of phenomena, however, are mere appearances, not truly existent events, and in your bewilderment you experience them as though they were real.

The bardo is not just the period between lives. In fact, the Buddha taught that as long as there is a state of bewilderment, all of samsara and nirvana without exception can be included in or summarized as the bardo. As long as there is fixation on duality, and as long as you believe in the independent existence of what you experience and the cognition that experiences it, you are in some kind of bardo or interval. As long as all of the different categories of "two's" arise for you—pleasure and pain, good and bad, samsara and nirvana—you are in the bardo. We conclude with the aspiration, "May I gain trust in the Buddha's teachings, that all of samsara and nirvana are in this way included in this category of bardo, which does not truly exist, but nevertheless appears to."

The bardo is divided into two aspects, the bardo of the true nature and the bardo of manner of appearance. "True nature" here means how things are, and "appearance" means how things seem or appear. "In absolute truth, things are beyond limit and their nature is the middle."

"Beyond limit" means beyond the limits of existence or absolute nonexistence, and beyond the limits of having a beginning or true origination and having an end or true cessation. The nature of things, absolute truth, is that middle which transcends all kinds of conceptual elaborations, including any concept about reality that you can come up with. The nature of things is beyond that and therefore is called "the middle" because it avoids any extreme. Therefore the nature of things actually is between or beyond all of your concepts and all of your dualism.

Your bewilderment starts with the fixation on duality—the duality of self and other, of pleasure and pain and so on—and it includes the appearance of self and other as separate. But the true nature of all of the things that appear to you as dual is not dual; it is beyond that, and in the words of the liturgy, it is between that. The nature of things that is between all extremes or limits is the *bardo of the absolute or true nature*. As the next line says, "Everything is that, and it is everything. There is nothing whatsoever that has any nature other than this." In a sense you can say that this nature is everything that there is, everything that truly exists, because it is the nature of all things. You end with the aspiration, "May I meet or see the face of the bardo of the true nature." "See the face" means not to merely understand the bardo, but to gain direct experience of it through precise instruction and the intensive practice of meditation and other methods.

The other aspect of the bardo is the bardo of how things appear. The term used here is *kündzop,* which is usually translated as "relative" or "relative truth," although it literally means "fake truth." Relative truth is fake truth because, when it is viewed by an undeluded cognition, it is seen to be unreal, to not truly exist. It is a process of bewilderment and bewildered appearances, and it is continuous in the sense that it is beginningless and it has never stopped. It is constantly gaining momentum, and its power is constantly increasing, causing your bewilderment to grow over time.

Through bewilderment you experience relative truth, or fake reality, as real. What is this like? It is like being in the audience of a skilled illusionist who, through some method or through the power of casting spells, can cause an audience to see all sorts of things that are not there. The illusionist can cause you to see people, horses, elephants, houses, whatever you want; none of these things are there, but as long as you do not realize that, you react to them with pleasure, pain, disappointment, happiness, enjoyment, fear, and so on, just as though they really were there. Your experience of relative truth is this beginningless deception by the fakery or illusion of your own bewilderment.

The term we usually translate as "existence" literally

means "possibility," so the next line says, "In this possibility, nothing is impossible."

The nature of existence is synonymous here with samsara, because it is founded on bewilderment and delusion. Because it is all of the nature of illusion and bewildered projections, anything is possible. Any form of bewilderment, any form of hallucination, can occur just as an illusionist can cause you to see just about anything. You end with the aspiration, "May I gain strong certainty about the bardo of how things appear."

In other words, you aspire to gain the certainty that all of the mere appearances—the projections of bewilderment that make up what we call relative truth or fake truth—are nothing more than the bewildered projections of a mind that is captivated by fixated belief in the duality of that which does not possess duality.

Next the text turns to a presentation of different aspects of the bardo. Initially it divides the bardo into three types, and then further divides the third of these into three intervals or phases. The first type of bardo is the interval in this life between birth and death, and it means exactly what it sounds like—the period of time that starts when you are born and ends when you start to die. What demarcates this interval, or separates it from the course of your existence, are physical events—the transformation of being born into a particular life and the decaying of that life, culminating in death. The experience of this interval between birth and death is also marked by physical activity and the physical transformations of all appearances—all of the things that you hear and say, positive and negative thoughts, pleasant and unpleasant experiences, and so on.

What needs to be understood about this first bardo, or interval, is that none of its appearances are reliable. They are ephemeral; they do not last and they are constantly changing. Ultimately speaking, the first type of bardo is a state of constant change, and the appearances of this life have no more existence than magical illusions or dreams. They are mere fluctuations and changes, not the persistent existence or abiding of anything. The aspiration connected with this first bardo, the interval between birth and death, is that you come to recognize all of the appearances of this life merely as the fluctuating hallucinations of a bardo. How do you do this? In the best case you practice intensive meditation until you can rest in even placement within the direct experience of the illusory nature of phenomena, the experience of emptiness that is their true nature. If you cannot do that, it is important at least to gain certainty, through examination, that the appearances of this life are ephemeral, illusory, and unreliable.

The second bardo that is described here is the interval that we normally call the dream state. This consists of appearances that do not really exist but that seem to exist because you are asleep. Because what we call sleep is a physical state, this interval, like the other one, is demarcated by physical changes. In this case the physical change is that when you fall asleep your senses stop functioning. You stop hearing, seeing, smelling, tasting, and feeling to a great extent, and therefore the images that arise in your mind take on an appearance of reality because there is no sense experience to overpower them. In dreams you seem to do all the things that you do while you are awake, and while you are dreaming you take these things to be really there. You think that you are actually seeing and hearing the things you seem to be seeing and hearing, but in fact you are not seeing or hearing anything. You are not doing anything. When you wake up, even though you realize that you were just dreaming, you further fixate on the appearances of the dream by investing them with significance. "Was it a good dream? Was it a bad dream? What does it mean?" In this way you solidify the illusory dream images even after you awake from them. Your primary bewilderment is thinking that a dream is real while you are dreaming, and your secondary bewilderment is thinking that the dream is important after you wake up. The aspiration here is to remove all of this bewilderment connected with the dream state. That is the express aspiration for the dream state, but by implication it applies to how you experience in general. Although you can distinguish the dream state from the waking state by the physical factor of sleep, in both states your cognition fundamentally functions in the same way: it is deluded, it is hallucinating. Once you are awake you can easily understand that the bewildered appearances of dreams are unreal, and if you think about it carefully, the bewildered appearances of the waking state are no more real. They are just like dreams or magical illusions in their unreliability, ephemerality, and impermanence. What this is really pointing out is that by eradicating the bewilderment of taking dreams as real, you can move as well toward eradicating the bewilderment of taking conventional waking appearances as real.

Interval of Possibility

The third interval is what is usually meant when people talk about the bardo and it is the principal subject of the rest of our text. It is the *interval of possibility* and is divided into three phases, simply called the first part, the middle part, and the last part, which correspond to dying, being dead, and approaching rebirth. These three are called the interval of possibility because this is the state in which the various possible rebirths can happen, as you will see.

There are three paths through which you prepare for the three phases of the interval of possibility. Through the *path of the clear light*, the nature of the first interval is recognized to be dharmakaya. Through the *path of the illusory body*, the nature of the second interval is realized to be sambhogakaya, the body of complete enjoyment. Through the *path of the nirmanakaya*, the final phase, the third interval, is transformed into rebirth as nirmanakaya. You initially make the aspiration, "May I traverse or complete these paths and thereby achieve liberation in these intervals."

Now what does this mean? You may say, "I meditate on

Mahamudra," or "I practice the Great Perfection," or "I meditate on the profound Middle Way," or you may say whatever it is you think you are doing. Whatever form of meditation you believe yourself to be practicing, what you are supposed to be doing in any of those three systems of practice is to come to a direct realization of the true nature of all things. In terms of what that nature is not, you could say that nature is not inherent existence. In terms of what it is, you could say it is the freedom from truly inherent or independent existence; it is the *clear light.*

The purpose of meditation in general is to gain the direct experience of the clear light and to gain sufficient experience to achieve liberation during the first phase of the interval at death. If you can realize that all things are empty of true existence, then that is the path that will bring liberation in the first interval.

In case that does not work, you can also meditate on pure appearances. That is to say that from within the state of emptiness, which is the nature of all things, the deity arises. This may involve the deity arising from a syllable, or from a scepter, and so on. Whatever deity it is—Vajravarahi, or any other—you identify yourself completely with this utterly unreal and yet absolutely vivid and pure clear appearance. By doing this in the second phase or interval you gain the possibility of liberation in the sambhogakaya of that deity.

In case that does not happen, you also prepare for taking a rebirth as emanation. This is to say that through the force of love and compassion, and the force of your aspirations for appropriate rebirth, you are able to stop inferior or inappropriate birth and choose a birth through which you can continue the path and be of benefit to others. That is how you achieve freedom of birth in the third and final phase of the interval of possibility.

This summarizes what is presented throughout the rest of the text, since the text is primarily concerned with the bardo as we usually mean it—the interval between lives.

THE FIRST PART: DYING

The first of the three parts of the interval of possibility consists of the entry into the clear light at the time of death. It
starts with the dissolution of the elements, which are qualities of physical matter such as solidity, cohesion and so on.
When your body starts to break down, which is what we
call dying, the elements start to fall apart or dissolve. They
are usually presented in the particular sequence given in this
text, although they do not always break down in the same
sequence. This standard sequence is based on the majority
of processes, but it can vary from person to person and is
not always the same.

When the earth element, the element of solidity, dissolves
or breaks down, you become unable to support your physical body. This is what happens, for example, as you get
older and become weaker. When the water element dissolves, the sense apertures like your eyes and nose start to
dry up. You start to have a dry mouth, and you do not have
enough natural fluids or moisture. When the fire element
dissolves, your temperature decreases and your warmth

starts to withdraw from the ends of the limbs inward, toward the center of your body. Then when the wind element dissolves, you stop breathing externally. This does not necessarily mean that you have become unconscious just yet. You may remain conscious, and your consciousness is still seated within your body, but at that point you stop breathing and your pulse comes to a halt. This is one place where the order can vary. A three-part process—*appearance, increase, and attainment*—follows the dissolution of the elements and precedes the entry into the clear light. It sometimes happens, however, that breathing has not stopped yet even while the person is experiencing both appearance and increase. We know this because individuals have described their experience of it as they are dying and while they are still able to talk, which means that they are still breathing. Nevertheless for clarity we use the classical sequence based on the experience of most dying people, which is that the four elements dissolve and are followed by appearance, increase, attainment, and then the clear light.

The *dissolution of appearances* is the first of the three stages that follow the dissolution of the elements. What happens to you as the dying person is that you see appearances subside and become a bright whiteness or white light that eventually is uniform. That appearance is associated with this stage, and there is a cognitive state that accompanies it. The accompanying cognitive state is that your awareness or mind becomes a little bit vague, like mist or smoke. This means, in this case, that sometimes you can focus and sometimes you cannot. Many people who are dying experience this, or at least start to experience it, before their breathing stops.

I knew an old lama in Darjeeling who, as he was dying, described all of this process up to this point and a little bit beyond it. Michael Doran, a staff member at KTD, definitely experienced the appearance stage before his breathing stopped, because as he was dying he said, "Where is all this light coming from?" This is not uncommon. When it happens, it means that the dying person is experiencing the dissolution of appearance. A third thing that happens along with the appearance stage is the suppression of a certain type of thinking. The thirty-three different forms of anger, or the thirty-three different aggressive thoughts—in short, all types of anger—stop. "Stop," however, means that they are suppressed. They become dormant. It does not mean that the dying person has purified the affliction of anger but that the physical condition of dying has shut down the biological mechanism that supports the emotion of anger, so anger is temporarily suppressed.

The next stage of the dying process is *augmentation* or *increase*. This refers to the increase of the appearance of death that arose during the previous stage. This stage also has an appearance, a cognitive aspect, and an aspect of suppression or dormancy. The appearance is that the dying person sees everything go red. Previously everything was white, and now everything becomes a uniform field of red. Cognition becomes like fireflies, which in this case means that it is sporadic; it flashes on, flashes off. Sometimes the mind is lucid, clear, and focused, and sometimes it is obscure. The suppression aspect is that when this stage of dying is reached, all forms of desire, lust, attachment, craving, hankering—any form of wanting, all of it—stops. Again, it has not been purified. The forty different types of desire are merely suppressed because of the biological dying process.

With the understanding that the order of sequence is indefinite to begin with, and because of the fact that the text says "most," we know that some people will realize that they are dying. Those who do realize it will also recollect what they have done. If they have led good and satisfying lives, then they will start to feel happy. If they have led lives full of harming others and so on, then they may start to be terrified. Often people at this point will start to have visions of their future parents and the place of their subsequent rebirth, along with different events or circumstances in their future life. For example, if the dying person can still speak at this point, it is known that butchers who kill animals and others who have harmed beings will have terrifying hallucinations that indicate their future rebirth. They may also sense things coming to get them and say something like, "Get these animals out of here, they are going to get me," and so on.

In short, the dying persons may become aware that they are dying and may also recollect their previous actions, and it is at this point that intervention is of the greatest benefit. What sort of intervention? At the point when appearance has dissolved into increase (the red appearance), the dying person's cognition can be steered somewhat. In other words, their mind is like fertile soil. Anything that is planted in it at that time can have a very powerful effect on what happens to them in the rest of the interval and therefore in their next life. At this point it is a good idea to recite the names and mantras of buddhas, the fathers and sons of the lineage, great gurus, and so on. Ideally the most powerful thing is for the person him or herself to actually recite these names and mantras, or at least bring them to mind. Otherwise, whoever is assisting them through the dying process can intervene by reciting these things with their mouth right next to or even touching the person's ear. In that way you try to remind them of those to whom they supplicate. You can also remind them of their previous practice, give them instructions, and so on. At this point the ejection of consciousness from the body can be performed for the person with the greatest benefit, because it is at this point that the consciousness can be ejected while it is still in the body and can be gotten hold of and moved. In summary, this is the critical time when interventions of all kinds will be of the greatest benefit.

We have looked at the stages of dissolution, the stages of dying, up through the first two of the three stages that precede the experience of the clear light—the stages of appearance and increase. The third stage that ensues upon or follows after increase is *attainment*. This is the final shutdown or dissolving of the physical processes of the living body that causes a corresponding set of experiences. Its appearance is utter blackness although there is not really the appearance of blackness; in fact, there is no appearance at all. Previously there was brilliant whiteness and then brilliant redness, and now there is the utter absence of appearances. This is happening because the functions of the body and mind that support or allow appearances are shutting down. The corresponding cognitive experience is that your awareness, your mind, becomes like a butter lamp in a vase. A butter lamp placed in a vase may be lit and burning and producing light, but none of the light will escape the vase.

From the outside it will appear to be just a dark vase. In the same way, there is a continued bare lucidity of cognition, but it is divorced from contact with any object that appears or that is cognitively apprehended. It is a state of mere lucidity without apprehension of any object, either with the senses or with the cognition itself.

The cognition is at the stage of the shutdown or dissolution process when the final seven of the eighty types of thoughts stop. Previously we saw the cessation of thoughts connected with the varieties of anger and the thoughts connected with desire. Now the last seven thoughts, which are the seven varieties of stupidity or bewilderment, cease. They do not stop in any final sense, but they are suppressed and become dormant. As with the previous two states of suppression, this suppression is caused by the simple fact that the biological processes that support them, and enable them to arise in connection with their respective objects, are simply not functioning at the moment. These thoughts stop, but they have not been purified; their tendency has not been in any way uprooted.

During this whole process of dissolution, there has been a gradual withdrawal of the cognitive faculties, which here refer to the six main functions of consciousness: the apprehension of visible forms by the eye consciousness, the apprehension of sounds by the ear consciousness, and in the same way the apprehension of smells, tastes, tactile sensations, and objects of mind. During the dissolution process, these six functions of mind or consciousness have gradually dissolved. All appearances—not only visual appearances, but also auditory and other appearances— have gradually diminished in intensity or clarity, and have finally disappeared altogether. This is something that you can often observe happening with the dying person. Sometimes while you are at their bedside the person will say, "Come closer, you are so far away." This is because they perceive you as being physically farther away from them than you are, simply because of what is happening to their eye consciousness. They will say, "Speak louder, I cannot hear you," because a corresponding thing is happening with the ear consciousness.

At the conclusion of the threefold shutdown of appearance, increase, and attainment, all of the elements of your conventional being, your body and mind, have become dormant. In other words your aggregates—your physical elements and your senses, all of these—have temporarily, in the words of our text, "entered the mandala of absolute truth." This means that they are temporarily absent as obscuring factors, although they have not been purified or uprooted. They are dormant, and because you are not seeing or hearing anything anymore, various hallucinations can arise at this point. People who have led nasty lives and done bad things will often have terrifying hallucinations that executioners, yamas, demonic beings, and so on are coming to get them. People who have led predominantly virtuous lives may have an experience of well-being, such as fleeting glimpses of pleasant environments, pleasant people, and so on. Remember that these appearances are like dreams. Because of the withdrawal of the consciousnesses, these hallucinations are entirely subjective. As is the case with dream images, they have no stability; they can fluctuate, change from one thing to another, and in any case do not last very long.

THE MOMENT OF DEATH:
EXPERIENCING THE CLEAR LIGHT

The shutting down processes conclude with the final events that constitute death. What keeps you alive—what keeps your mind biologically seated in your physical body—is a wind or energy that is called *life wind*. The life wind abides within the avadhuti or central channel of your body. You know that the conditions for becoming a biological being were the ovum from your mother and the sperm from your father. The original seeds that led to your resultant physical being are still present within your body. They are held in place by the life wind, and they also contain the life wind and keep it in the body. The way this works is as follows: The remaining seed essence of the ovum is the *red element*, and while you are alive it is in the center of your body below your navel. The seed essence of your father's sperm is the *white element*, and it is present in the center of your body at the very top of your head. These seed essences are both held in place and forced apart by the life wind that fills the central channel between them. The central channel is inflated by the life wind in the way that a tire is inflated by the air within it. Not only does the life wind maintain the seed essences at the upper and lower ends of the central channel, but because they are trapped in those places the seed essences also contain the life wind between them and keep it from escaping.

What happens with the shutdown of everything is that the life wind, which is the most basic factor of your being alive in the conventional sense, is the last to shut down. As it shuts down, it withdraws into the heart area. What happens is similar to deflation except that the central channel does not actually deflate; the pressure within it is withdrawn. As a result, the red and white elements move for the first time. The red element that you received from your mother rises up because there is nothing forcing it down. It rises up toward and eventually comes to rest in your heart. At the same time, the white element that you received from your father descends or falls down from the top of your head until it also reaches your heart. The end result is that the five things that form the essence of your being come together in one place. The most basic mind, which is the all-basis consciousness; the life wind, which previously filled the entire central channel; and all of the potential cognitive functions—those three along with the white and red elements, come together at the very center of your heart in the midst of the central channel. This is the actual moment of death.

When these essences of your being come together, and because all possible types of thoughts or conceptuality have ceased and are temporarily dormant, you have an experience that is a cognitive experience, not a sensory experience. In quality this is like the experience of a boundless, clear, and cloudless sky. It is the experience of the *fundamental or ground clear light*. What you experience at this moment is not because of any meditation you may have done previously. You experience it because it is your true nature, and it is experienced at this point in the death process not only by people, but also even by small insects. It is experienced simply because all beings have buddha nature. What you are experiencing at this point is buddha nature itself.

The reason why you can experience buddha nature under those circumstances, and that you do not experience it normally, is that normally it is masked by thought. Because all thought has ceased and become dormant at this point, there is nothing to mask the experience of buddha nature. That's the good news. The bad news is that, unless you have trained yourself assiduously in recognizing the clear light during your preceding life, you will not recognize it. Everybody experiences the clear light, but obviously that is not sufficient. If you do not have enough experience in recognizing it, you will be stunned. You will be like a small child looking at the murals in a temple. When a child looks at a mural, they see the same colors and shapes that an adult does, but they have no way to recognize them as depictions of one thing or another. They cannot make the judgment, "This is well painted; that is ill painted." Nor can they think, "Here is this deity, there is that deity," and so on. They are completely ignorant of what they are seeing. In the same way, if you have not familiarized yourself through practice with the clear light during your preceding life, it will not do you any good to see it now. The ground clear light will appear to you as it does to each and every sentient being at the moment of death and you will experience it;

nevertheless you will not recognize it, and it will only last a moment. You will move from that experience to the next one in a moment. "Moment" here does not necessarily mean a specific unit of time like a finger snap. Here it means the duration of an action that is uninterrupted by any other action. For the time that you are immersed in the experience of the clear light, you remain immersed in it; however, failing to recognize it, your mind emerges and moves on to something else, and it is finished.

Therefore what is necessary, above and beyond all else, is to familiarize yourself with the clear light during your lifetime. This is done through hearing, reflection, and above all through meditation. By understanding what will happen at death and the process that you will go through, you can prepare yourself to recognize the clear light. By cultivating the faculties of recollection and alertness through meditation practice, especially meditation practice based upon the profound instructions of your guru, you can develop the faculties of mindfulness and alertness that will enable you to recognize the ground clear light when it arises.

You do this by meditating upon the traditions that teach you how to meditate on the clear light: the Middle Way, the Mahamudra, or the Great Perfection. In any one of these you go through a series of practices that culminate in the ability to experience the clear light to some degree in this life. What you experience as a meditation practitioner is the *path clear light* or the *child clear light*, and it is something that is experienced through conscious and assiduous cultivation. Only through such cultivation do you have a chance of recognizing the fundamental or natural mother clear light at the time of death. The aim of these meditation practices,

EXPERIENCING THE CLEAR LIGHT

and the entire systems that culminate in these practices, is to rest in a state free of all mental elaboration, and in that way to gain familiarity with the path or child clear light. At the time of death, because you are familiar with it, you will recognize the ground or fundamental clear light, the *mother clear light*, just as you would recognize someone you had seen before.

Seeing the child clear light is analogous to seeing a modern photograph. Just as there is a difference between a photograph of someone and the actual person, likewise there is a difference between the cultivated child clear light and the actual mother clear light. If you have seen a good photograph of someone, you can later recognize the person from having seen the photograph. In the same way, if you cultivate an authentic experience of the path clear light in this life, you can recognize the ground clear light at the moment of death.

Practice of the meditative state that cultivates the clear light during this lifetime is marked by three characteristics: well-being, lucidity, and no-thought or nonconceptuality. The way we normally experience the clear light is quite imperfect, because in this life it is fleeting and because it manifests only to a certain degree and not beyond that. You experience some degree of well-being, some degree of lucidity, and some degree of freedom from conceptualization. The ground clear light that you experience at the moment of death, however, is endowed with these three characteristics to the ultimate degree. It is endowed with absolute well-being, which is perfect bliss. It is utter and pure lucidity, and it is totally and completely free of thought or conceptuality of any kind. These characteristics make it so different from your normal state of mind that, in order to recognize it, you must cultivate a meditative state endowed to some extent with these same three characteristics. Therefore in this life you have to cultivate *child luminosity*, which is a one-pointed samadhi or meditative absorption endowed with the characteristics of the ground clear light itself.

The *ground clear light* is called the "fundamental or basic clear light," the "mother clear light," and the "natural clear light." It is called these three things because it is the true nature of all things. It is, in and of itself, utterly and completely pure, and it has been utterly and completely pure and perfect from the very beginning. In fact, it is indestructible. It is unaffected by anything, and it is utterly unchanging. It never has changed, never does change, and never will change. The only change is whether or not it is experienced and whether or not it is recognized when experienced. If you have cultivated a familiarity with the child clear light during your preceding life, then when the ground clear light appears, it is like a child recognizing his or her mother. This is the *meeting of the mother and child clear lights*. At that point you both experience the true and natural clear light and also recognize it based on your cultivated experience. What you previously experienced and what you experience at that moment mix together like water being poured into water. This is the best type of liberation, *liberation at the moment of death*. In a sense you could call this the beginning of the bardo, because it is the first interval, but it is also known as *before the interval*. It is the first opportunity for liberation and it is liberation in dharmakaya, to be achieved by those of the highest capacity who have familiarized themselves with the clear light.

It is important to understand that this type of liberation, when someone recognizes the ground clear light at the moment of death, is complete and full. It is the actual achievement of perfect awakening, or buddhahood, at the moment of death. When a person achieves this type of liberation, they achieve buddhahood with all of the qualities for which it is renowned—not only their own liberation, but the ensuing and permanent all-pervasive ability to be of consummate benefit to others in every possible way until each and every other being has likewise achieved perfect awakening. Recognizing the value of attempting to achieve such a state of awakening and liberation through the recognition of the ground clear light at death, you should abandon all the distractions of this life. Distractions refer to all of the things with which you normally concern yourself—things that are of no use whatsoever, either immediately or in the long-term, or that are actually destructive and negative. You should even abandon things that at best are of only temporary and largely physical benefit. Such things are distractions because involvement with them prevents you from engaging in the type of assiduous practice that is necessary to achieve this liberation and awakening. In order to achieve it you have to abandon distractions and abide in solitude. This means practicing in isolation like Jetsun Milarepa and remaining in a state of threefold stillness.

Threefold stillness means that your body is utterly still. It is free from unnecessary movement of any kind and especially from unnecessary and meaningless physical activity. Stillness of speech means that you are silent. Your faculty of speech is undisturbed by the meaningless babble of conventional speech. Stillness of mind means that your mind is in a state free of elaboration. This refers not merely to the state of tranquillity, or shinay, but to a state of insight in which your mind is withdrawn from all forms of thought or conceptual elaboration. In short, in order to experience and thereby be able to recognize the clear light, you have to cultivate a meditative state that is the conjunction of lucidity and emptiness without fixation.

Your mind is defined by the fact that you can cognize. You can experience, you are aware, and therefore the defining characteristic of your mind is cognitive lucidity. Your mind is not just lucidity because it is not a substantial brilliance like the sun or the moon. The mind, while lucid, is utterly insubstantial. It is empty of any substance or entity whatsoever. Furthermore, this lucidity and this emptiness are not two different things. They are inseparable. You rest in a state in which you experience your mind just as it is, which is the union of lucidity and emptiness, and you do so without any kind of fixation, without any conceptualized apprehension. This is *great even-placement*. In general, even-placement can refer to either the meditation of perfect tranquillity or of insight. Here it refers to insight because it is more than a state of tranquillity. In this state the mind is resting completely and utterly within a direct experience of its own nature. You remain within that state, practicing the *conduct of extreme simplicity*, which refers to a mode of conduct that is free from elaborations or complexities. Your mind is free not only from mundane activities, distractions, and disturbances, but even from conceptual functions of mind and thinking itself. At this point you make the aspiration to perfect this practice—the conduct of extreme simplicity—so that you can achieve the supreme liberation, perfect awakening, at the very moment of death.

This kind of liberation is not purely legendary. It is not the case that we can speak of this liberation by saying, "People used to achieve this in the good old days, but nowadays it does not happen." In fact, it happens all the time. In my lifetime—more specifically, since I left Tibet—there have been several instances of this in my own experience and countless others as well. When I was thirty-eight years old, there was a certain tutor of a Drukpa Kagyu lama called Gar Rinpoche. This tutor passed away at the refugee camp in Buxador where we were all living. In order to understand what happened to him and to his body, you need to understand that he had been very sick and feeble before he died; yet just before his death, he sat up perfectly straight, seeming completely comfortable and at ease. He dismissed the attendants who had been helping him, saying, "You all go outside and play," then asked for his outer robe and his meditation hat. When they were brought to him, he put them on and started to do his daily practice book. He chanted the first half of it, and in that state he passed away, leaving the second half undone. Having died, he remained in a state of meditative absorption for three days.

This happened at a time when it was extremely hot in Buxador. As you know, dead bodies rot and stink very quickly in hot weather, but his did not. For the three days of his samadhi, he remained seated upright, without the slightest appearance of decay, either visible or olfactory. In fact, the room was hot not only because of the time and location, but because people were offering butter lamps, as many as a hundred, in the room where his body was left. Still, the double heat from the lamps still did not cause any scent of decay. As for how he looked, we know that, generally speaking, when someone dies, their complexion is no longer rosy, to say the least. But the lama's complexion actually improved. He looked more florid, more lively, after death than he had while he was alive.

These indications, specifically the appearance of circulation, the florid complexion, and the lack of decay, are considered definite signs that someone has achieved liberation in the dharmakaya and perfect buddhahood at the moment of death. Another example of this was a retreat master that I knew who passed away in the same way and remained seated with the same signs for the same period of three days. There was also a lama called Karma Norbu who had done a retreat at Palpung Monastery and was a disciple of Chatral Rinpoche. He lived in an isolated place in Nepal, in a small house where water was scarce, causing disputes between him and his neighbors. Yet when he died, a multicolored light, like the light of a rainbow, started to emerge from his body and from his house, filling the surrounding area. It was also noticed that his body was getting a little bit smaller as time went on. His neighbors of course recognized this as what it was and felt somewhat regretful about their having fought with him in the past. Now they prostrated to his remains and venerated him properly.

Lama Ganga, a lama who lived for some time in the West, passed away at Thrangu Monastery and after his death remained seated in samadhi for no less than five days. I saw that myself because I was there when he died. My point is that there are many instances up to the present day of people achieving perfect awakening through these means. In fact, it happens so commonly and people are so used to it that they do not even bother to report it every time. They simply say, "Well that's what happens if you practice dharma. That's dharma's blessing." But you should consider what it is and not be so casual about it, because it is definite and irrefutable proof of the possibility of perfect awakening at the moment of death.

I mention all of this and comment on it at length because it is important to understand that, as bad as the times are, the dharma is not affected or diminished in any way. We do indeed live in an age of decadence, but the dharma is not decadent. The dharma is the same as it always has been. The land of Tibet has suffered greatly throughout the preceding century, yet all that has happened there—all that has bought great suffering to the people and has greatly diminished practice resources—has not affected the power or authenticity of dharma in any way. The compassion of buddhas and bodhisattvas and their blessings are utterly unaffected by the circumstances of the times we live in. The dharma is always effective and it will always work. You simply have to do it. I am confident that if someone practices these things properly, they will definitely achieve the result described here. It is infallible. I want to inspire you with this same confidence and knowledge that, "If I practice this, I will achieve this."

It is that simple, and it is that infallible, because your basic nature is the ground clear light. That is your true being. The only other thing that is necessary for you to achieve awakening is to familiarize yourself with your basic nature through meditation on the path clear light. The big question is whether someone does or does not meditate assiduously on the path clear light during their life. That obviously depends upon being taught how to do so, which in turn obviously depends on having access to a spiritual friend. If you have no access to a spiritual friend and receive no instruction, you will not do any meditation and therefore you will not achieve liberation and awakening. Once you have access to the spiritual friend, and once you have access to instruction on how to cultivate familiarity through meditation with the path clear light, you simply have to do it. If you do it assiduously enough, achieving liberation and awakening at the moment of death is a certainty.

THE MIDDLE PART: BEING DEAD

If you have not achieved sufficient familiarity with the clear light during the immediately preceding life, then you will not recognize the ground clear light at the moment of death. The moment after it appears you will move on to the second phase of the bardo. This is the main part of the interval of possibility, and, as we have seen, it is what most people think of when they use the term *bardo*. Previously, collected together at the moment of death at one place in the center of your heart were your all-basis consciousness, the remnant of the life wind, the potential for other cognitive functions, and the white and red drops. If you did not recognize the ground clear light at that time, these five separate again, and two of them leave your body. These two— the basic consciousness and the life wind together—leave your body through one or another of nine apertures: the navel, the place between the eyebrows, the aperture at the top of the head, the nose, the ears, the mouth, the eyes, the anus, or the urethra. The basic consciousness is mixed with or riding the life wind. It will leave your body from any one of those apertures, and once it has left it will not go back in. It is as soon as the consciousness leaves your body that the appearances of the interval proper start to arise. "Starting from that point onward, you have the appearance of your subsequent body."

It is put this way because the text is, after all, very brief. When presented in more detail, what is usually explained is that, for the first half of the period of the interval, you will appear to yourself to have the body you had in the preceding life. For the second half you will appear to have the body you are going to have in your subsequent life. The reason for this is that this appearance is a purely mental body. It is made from habit. You initially have the appearance of your preceding body because that is what you are used to. That is what you expect. On the other hand, the karma that put you in your preceding life and kept you in that life is exhausted. It was used up, and that is why you died. Therefore the karmically bound habit of that life will lose momentum or diminish during the period in the interval.

What happens is that initially you have a very vivid impression of having the same body you had before. In other words, you think of yourself as the person you thought you were before. For example, I would consider myself to be Karthar, thinking, "I have Karthar's body," and so on. That body will appear at the beginning, but as the interval continues it will start to become less distinct, more vague. Then after the middle of the forty-nine days, which is the usual period of the interval, you will start to have an initially vague and then more and more vivid impression of having your future body.

In either case, whichever body you appear to possess, the

body has certain characteristics. Do not forget, it is utterly illusory. It is like a magical illusion, a hypnotic image, or some other hallucination. Therefore, in a sense, this body is independent. It did not grow, and it was not produced by anything, so it is independent of physical causes. It is also independent of most physical conditions. It is different from your present body in that whatever is particularly wrong with or defective in your present body will appear to have been restored. If one of your legs has been amputated, for example, you will get that body part back. If one or more of your senses is malfunctioning—if you only have one working eye or you cannot hear with one of your ears—you will appear, in the bardo, to get that function back.

Bardo beings never seem to have defective senses. Of course, they do not have physical sense organs at all, which is why this is the case. They appear to themselves and to other interval beings to have a full set of the senses of their particular species. Because they have only a mental body, they can pass through solid matter the way a fly passes through a beam of sunlight. Flies can buzz their way through a beam of light without being in any way impeded by it, and in the same way, as an interval being, you can fly through solid matter, even the hardest rock. It is not that you have miraculous powers; it is simply that your body is purely mental, and the mind can go anywhere, do anything. It does not require physical or verbal effort or exertion. This being the case, as an interval being you will find yourself instantly in any place you think of.

From one point of view you could say this is miraculous, but do not forget that it is impulsive. It is spontaneous in the negative sense of the word because it is not under control.

You are driven about by whatever occurs to you, and there is no physical body to prevent you from being instantly driven to another place. Having no physical body, interval beings cannot use clothing and cannot eat food. They do still have the habit of hunger and thirst, and they suffer from it, but they cannot eat or drink. They can only consume scents, but they cannot be nourished by just any smell. The only smells that they can actually experience as nourishment are the scents of substances consecrated to them. It is therefore good to burn consecrated herbs and edible substances together, and to specifically dedicate them to beings in the interval. This is why, especially when dealing with a recently deceased person, we perform a *singed offering* in the evening as a regular daily observance. This consists of singeing consecrated substances and other edibles and dedicating them to beings in the interval and to others.

Who can see these beings? They can see themselves and they can see one another. A being in the interval can see other interval beings, but normally we cannot see them. The exception to this are individuals who have achieved the divine eye through meditative prowess and the interval beings who themselves have a limited form of this. Bardo beings may have a certain type of supercognition, but it is not necessarily as good as it sounds, because it also is compulsive and impulsive. For example, an interval being might know that something is going on such as a dharma teaching, and they might go there, but their response to it will not necessarily be positive.

Once you have been in the interval long enough to start to assume the appearance of your subsequent body rather than your previous body, there are clues as to where you are going to be born. Aside from appearing as whatever species you will be, clues are also given by your spatial position. Beings who are going to be reborn in a higher state—as humans, devas, or asuras—will be moving upward and will generally be facing upward, with the head facing the sky rather than the ground. Beings that are going to be reborn in a lower state—as animals, pretas, or hell beings—will generally be facing downward and moving downward. Because interval beings have no physical bodies and therefore no basis for the perception of physical light, they do not see the sun and moon. They can experience an environment similar to ours and appear to be in a place, but they will see no light from the sun and moon, and their bodies will cast no shadows.

Now the pure appearances of dharmata arise. The consciousness of the deceased person has emerged from the body after the person has failed to recognize the ground clear light, and the *intermediate existence* has begun. The pure appearances of dharmata will consist especially of the appearances of the peaceful and wrathful deities. These are the forty-two peaceful deities, the fifty-eight wrathful deities, and the pure vidyadharas. They arise after your consciousness has left your body, and they appear to emerge from the body. Although they are part of you, they seem to have become separate from you as they left your body. They appear as if they are in front of you or external, and they arise as magnificent deities. They are sambhogakayas, or bodies of complete enjoyment, with their respective appearances, both peaceful and wrathful. They are very bright, brilliant, and surrounded by intolerably bright light of many colors. In fact, the reason you do not achieve liberation upon their appearance in general is the intolerable brilliance of their light.

At the same time, five other types of light are appearing, and these represent the six states that are the pathways to the five types of rebirth. Because these five other lights are types of birth rather than species, the five types of rebirth do not include the jealous gods. The five types of rebirths are devas, humans, animals, pretas, and hell beings. The species *asura*, or jealous gods, can consist as two beings or types of rebirth, which are in some cases devas and in other cases animals. The lights that are the pathways to all of those rebirths are white, red, yellow, and blue, followed by very, very dark or dim blue that is almost darkness or nonexistent. The sequence of colors is not always absolutely consistent, but the point is that the worse the realm, the less brilliant the light. The reason for this is that the light of the pure appearances—which can be white, yellow, red, blue, or green—is very, very bright. It is so intolerably bright that you may perceive it as threatening, dangerous, and destructive, and run from it. The lights of the six realms, representing the five pathways to rebirth, are all muted, and very soothing in appearance. Because of karma, if you find the wisdom lights irritating and terrifying, you may choose instead the soothing light of one of the six states. Even worse, because the lights of the lower states are more soothing than the lights of the higher states, rebirth in lower states predominates over rebirth in higher states.

Therefore what you want to do if you get to this part of the interval, which is the beginning of the second phase, is to choose the threatening, brilliant, vivid lights over the soothing, muted ones. In order to do this, you need to prepare by reflecting during your lifetime that the really, really bright scary lights, the brilliant ones, are the wisdom ones, and that the soothing, muted ones lead at least to samsara and probably to lower states. Initially you will probably just see the rays of brilliant lights and not the deities, and the rays in their brilliance and sharpness will seem to be like weapons to you. It is important to prepare for that experience because if you choose the path of a wisdom light, you will achieve liberation in its respective realm. If you choose the path of one of the samsaric lights, as we all evidently did, you know what happens.

At this stage you have a mental body that seems to be the body you had in your last life. Although this body may have restored senses, you will not immediately recognize that it is different from your physical body. Nevertheless it is important to prepare yourself to recognize the signs that indicate that you are dead. That is important because, obviously, the first prerequisite in choosing what to do in the interval is to know that you are in the interval. If you do not know that, then you will not make the right choices. What are the signs that you are in the interval? Generally, the signs are the appearance of sounds and forms that are utterly unfamiliar. Most of these are pretty scary, and they get scarier and scarier as it goes on. You hear scary sounds like a billion thunderclaps at once, and you see forms of different sorts of beings, not just wisdom deities but also terrifying beings the size of huge mountains, and so on. You see and hear all sorts of scary things that you have never seen before. You become more and more agitated, which means that the chance of liberation tends to decrease over this period. The point is that you need to recognize when you are in the interval, and to do so you must cultivate a familiarity with the signs that you are there. Having recognized them, you need to make the right choice, which is the path of the five wisdoms, not the paths of the five types of samsaric rebirth. If you do not know that you are in the interval, you will not choose one of the five wisdom lights, and you will just go with instinct, which will lead you towards the soothing lights and samsara.

The interval experience continues, and time passes with you in a mental body. Since your mind is not in any way restrained or governed by the solidity of a physical body, you become more and more anxious and agitated. As in life, you respond to anxiety with kleshas, and your kleshas grow in intensity as the interval continues. They can become like a blazing fire that totally possesses you. Do not forget that you are also blown about by the wind of your previous actions, which arise in the form of impulsive thoughts that send you from one place to another without your control. As your anxiety and kleshas increase, this experience becomes more and more turbulent, worse and worse. You have less and less leisure to think about anything. You become more frightened and saddened, and the hallucinations degenerate. You start to become more and more frightened, see more and more frightening things, respond to them more and more with anxiety and kleshas, and so on. Unless you have cultivated a preparation and familiarity with what is going to happen, you are simply unprepared to deal with it, and you have no control over what is happening. You are just blown about and there is nothing really to help you; you are buffeted about by the violent wind of your own karma. Here "wind" should be understood to be metaphoric, not a literal wind. It means the force of impulses born from previous actions that throw you uncontrollably about from place to place and experience to experience. Normally, being buffeted about in that way is the principal experience of the second phase of the interval.

At the same time, this is the point when we talk about liberation through hearing in the bardo or interval. Through hearing about opportunities for liberation in this phase, you have the opportunity to choose the lights of the five wisdoms over the muted lights of the five types of samsaric rebirth, and thereby achieve liberation. It is important to familiarize yourself with and prepare yourself for these experiences because the opportunities for liberation in this phase of the interval can only be taken advantage of by someone who has heard about them.

Since the interval state is considered a state of being, it has a duration or life span that we generally classify as forty-nine days, since that seems to be the length of that interval for most beings. For the first three-and-a-half days after death, and after the passing and nonrecognition of the ground clear light, the consciousness of the deceased person will probably still be within their body. Until the consciousness departs from the body, the person is largely unconscious. They may be sporadically conscious, but even when conscious they are still extremely confused, like someone who is intoxicated or drunk. Eventually whether it does so immediately after the failure to recognize the ground clear light or after three-and-a-half days, the consciousness emerges from the body, and the person starts to have the experiences and hallucinations that characterize the second phase of the interval.

For some or much of the time in this phase, the deceased persons will not know that they are dead. (I could call the interval being "it" rather than "he or she," because it no longer has gender, but that's rude, so I will say "they.") At times you may suspect that you are dead, but basically you will not have any more certainty that you are dead and in the bardo than you normally have when you are dreaming. Therefore you will be extremely agitated by all of the strange things that keep happening to you. You encounter beings that you have never seen before and hear sounds that you have never heard before. You do not know where you are and why you are there, and all of the agitation around you, all the rushing about and so on, will be extremely disturbing. You will still see those that you loved, friends, family, and others, and you will try to communicate with them. Because you do not know that you are an interval being, you see no reason why, when you speak to someone, you should not be answered. Of course, you are not answered because you are not visible. You become frustrated and aggrieved every time you try to talk to one of your relatives or friends and they ignore you. Eventually you begin to figure out the reason why. You start to understand that you are dead, but as soon as you figure that out, you react even more strongly.

For example, when you see your former aggregates—it is polite to say "aggregates," but what it means is "corpse"— you will try to get back into that body, because you identify with it so strongly. You will not be able to get back into your body, but you will still be very attached to it and to how it is treated. You will be very upset, of course, by seeing your dead body, and distressed to see your relatives and loved ones crying and grieving and so on. When you see people making arrangements for the disposal of your wealth and belongings, and you see your stuff being divvied up, you will not like it.

Your attitude towards your former aggregates (i.e., your corpse) will alter over time for much the same reason that your identification with the mental body of habit alters. The perception of yourself as your preceding body starts to weaken and is superseded by a perception of your subsequent body. Although you were initially attached to your corpse, eventually the karma of being in that body will be over, and gradually the habit left behind by that karma will weaken. Eventually you will start to dislike the corpse, and finally you will be happier when you do not see it and you will want it to be disposed of. You are still attached enough to your body that you will get very upset when it is disposed of, for example when it is cremated or buried or cast into water. You will become especially angry when people are disrespectful of your body by calling it a "corpse." If we speak the way we do of dead bodies saying, "Well, that thing is a corpse. It is not so-and-so, it is just their dead body," you will not like it. You will still have enough identification with that body as part of yourself that you will be as upset as you would have been if someone had said something about your body while you still inhabited it.

Eventually, having realized that you are dead, you will attempt to comfort your loved ones who are grieving for you. You will say, "Don't worry, don't worry, I'm right here. Can't you see me? I'm right here." Of course, your loved ones cannot see you, so you will be saddened by your inability to comfort your grieving survivors, and you too will start to grieve and cry. You may get to the point of fainting, or almost fainting, through grief and frustration. On the other hand, when you see people who are not grieving, you will be angry about that. You will resent people who dislike you, make jokes about you and laugh, or are otherwise disrespectful about you, now that you are dead. You will feel that some people just do not care that you are dead; they are laughing about something else or playing and entertaining themselves, and in general they are going about their lives normally. You will think, "How can they do that when I'm in this state? I've just been pulled right out of my body! I'm wandering in the bardo! I'm going through all of this, but they are laughing and having a good time and I can't communicate with them!"

As an interval being, you will actually feel enmity for those people, even though they may be persons you did not even know. You will resent those who are not grieving as much as you are distressed by those who are mourning. When you see the disposition of your possessions, especially those that were particularly valuable or precious, you will resent it. When others make use of your former belongings, you will think, "This stuff was worth a lot to me. I put a lot into it, and now this person is wasting it." You will be very angry about that, and you will actually follow the stuff around after it is passed on. The dead person's consciousness will often be attracted to the site of their former possessions. This is one reason why soon after someone died in Tibet it was customary to offer at least a certain amount of their treasured possessions to the Three Jewels to help the dead person cut through their attachment to their previous belongings and to prevent these things being used in a way that would upset them.

If you have no instructions to follow, and have not been taught how to prepare for the bardo, you will experience the appearances of the interval of possibility in much the same way you experience the dream state. You will have very little basis for knowing what is going on, just as you are pretty well lost when you are dreaming. Because the average or untrained person will not know for some time that they are dead, they will be at the mercy of the events that appear to occur. They believe that they are real just in the same way that they do not know when they are dreaming. If you do not understand what you are undergoing, what you are seeing and hearing, you will be totally at the mercy of your bewilderment and the bewildered appearances. Therefore the aspiration says, "May I train myself in dream, which is the manner of appraisal of the path."

This refers to the practice of dream that is part of the six dharmas of Naropa and similar systems, in which you train to develop the consistent ability to dream lucidly. This means knowing that you are dreaming while you are dreaming so that thereafter you can transform the dream state from impure appearances to pure appearances. The practice of lucid dreaming exists largely because it is the best preparation for this phase of the interval. As long as you do not know you are dreaming when you are asleep, you are not going to know that you are dead when you are dead. In order to recognize that you are dead and in the interval, you need to be able to recognize when you are dreaming and asleep. To transform the appearances that occur at this stage of the interval—the principal method here—you need to be able to transform the appearances of dreams as well.

You need to prepare yourself by having a certain attitude towards conventional waking state appearances, because in order to gain skill in dreaming, you need to gain skill in relating to conventional appearances. Fundamentally this consists of learning to constantly view all the appearances of the daytime waking state as illusory, like magical illusions. You need to reinforce and maintain this attitude until it gets to the point where the emptiness of appearances actually becomes an object of direct experience, and the appearances manifest to you spontaneously and clearly, without your having to reinforce them with the thought that they are devoid of inherent existence. The attitude of regarding appearances as illusory needs to be reinforced throughout the waking state until conceptual reinforcement is no longer necessary, and you do not need to remind yourself that appearances are empty. When you develop such a momentum or continuity of mindfulness and certainty, it becomes not merely something you are telling yourself; it is the truth. You are certain about the emptiness of appearances, and they actually appear to you that way. Your aspiration is, "May I reach the point where wisdom has been attained."

Here wisdom specifically means the state of mind in which you directly see appearances as the unity of appearance and emptiness. Reaching that state is the prerequisite for gaining mastery over the dream state, and eventually the interval state as well. What prevents us from doing this? What are the main obstacles that impede cultivation of awareness during the waking state, during the dream state, and therefore and most importantly, during the interval state as well? They are the *three thieves* that steal from you any chance of liberation, any chance of getting out of samsara. The first of these is doubt, which in this case means questions such as, "Are appearances empty or not? Is this the interval, or is it not?" Doubt will prevent the faculty of mindfulness from being strong enough and focused enough to cut through the illusion of appearances. It is doubt that causes us constantly to reenter the samsaric cycle, and it is doubt that prevents us from gaining the momentum necessary to break out of it.

The second thief is fixation on reality, meaning the fixation that appearances are what they appear to be. Fixating that this is truth or reality is maintained by doubt, and doubt prevents us from putting a stop to the fixation. All of the habits of reacting to appearances as if they were real will arise again, generating kleshas and so on. Whether it is during this life or during the interval after death, kleshas will re-arise because you think these appearances are real and therefore you react to them in that way.

The third thief is mindlessness. This means lack of recollection of what you are attempting to keep in mind, such as the illusoriness of appearances, the fact that you are in the interval, and so on. It is mindlessness, the lack of recollection, that keeps us lost at sea, wandering endlessly. The aspiration here is, "May I become free from these three thieves who steal from me the opportunity of liberation from samsara."

Next we discuss the essential means by which you can achieve liberation in the second phase of the interval and the reason why this phase is called the "opportunity of liberation." Using the means of transforming the appearance of your mental body into the body of the deity, you can achieve liberation in the sambhogakaya. This method depends upon practice in your preceding life, because it consists of employing, in the interval after death, the principal method of mantra or Vajrayana. This is the most profound of all paths and, if practiced in the preceding life and properly employed, it can bring liberation at this point.

The details of this path consist, first, of the actual transformation of all appearances—the appearance of your mental body and all other appearances—into the rainbowlike vajra body of the deity. Secondly, the perception of all sounds is transformed into the mantra of the deity, the vajra sound that is the unity of sound and emptiness. This is significant because, in this interval especially, there are terrifying sounds—very loud sounds, like a billion thunderclaps heard simultaneously—and these are so disturbing that you need a means or method by which to alter your perception of them. Thirdly, your perceptions, and therefore the experience of your mind itself, are transformed into the vajra mind, which is the mind that is the unity of bliss and emptiness.

The aspiration here is to train to become skilled in the means of mantra, and thereafter have the opportunity to employ in the interval the three essential points that make up the principal feature of the most profound path. If these are employed, what happens is that the mental body of the being in the interval is transformed. As we have seen, this mental body is composed of the life wind from the previous body and the subtle mind, or all-basis consciousness. In other words, this mental body that is composed purely of wind-mind is transformed, through the interval being's perception of it, into the illusory body in the form of the deity.

The practitioner, who has assumed the illusory body of the deity, further purifies their mental body by immersing their mind in the clear light. When the illusory body in the form of the deity is in that way purified by the fire of the clear light, it becomes the body of great unity, which is endowed with the best of all aspects. "Best of all aspects" means emptiness that is at the same time great bliss. Here the miraculous body of great unity refers to an illusory body that is inseparable from the purifying clear light. Otherwise put, this is the body of a deity in which the form and wisdom of the deity are united, inseparable. Thus the final aspiration of this phase is, "May I achieve the sambhogakaya in this second or principal phase of the interval of possibility."

THE LAST PART: APPROACHING REBIRTH

In the second phase we saw there was opportunity for achieving liberation in the interval through the transformation of your mental body into the sambhogakaya of your deity. This obviously depends upon assiduous practice in the preceding life and on having received instruction. Most beings who find themselves in the second interval do not achieve liberation there because they have not done the preparation or even received the instruction that would enable them to do it. If the being does not achieve liberation in the second interval, the third interval will begin.

The difference between the second and the third phases of the bardo is that the third phase is said to begin at the point where the habits from your preceding life have weakened so much that you begin to identify primarily with the body of the next life. As a result, you are looking for a body and a place to find birth, and you feel extremely lost. The defining characteristic of the third phase of the interval of possibility is that you are obsessively searching for a birthplace, and that is the principal practice in this third phase.

You are trying to avoid a conventional, compulsive birth where you would be put into a birthplace under the compulsion of your karma and karmic impulses.

At this point, not only have you lost your previous physical body, but also the habit of it has waned to the point where you feel extremely vulnerable. You feel like a traveler who cannot find a hotel or place to stay. As a more compelling analogy, you are like a warrior in the midst of battle who has fallen off your horse and is trying to remount it or even to get back onto any horse. That is the sort of urgency that you feel at this point in the interval, so it is here that you are particularly subject to the compulsion to be reborn. Here birthplace does not necessarily mean a geographical location; it means the container for the consciousness. It can mean the womb if you are going to be born in a womb, but it depends on what the species is.

When you start to look for the birthplace, certain indications can show what sort of birth you are moving toward. When those who are going to be reborn as devas or gods start searching for a birthplace, they find themselves amidst the god realm, and they are attracted to it. They see wealth and luxury, and they like it and want to stay there. There will be indications of this in the body they have left behind. If someone is moving toward a god or deva rebirth, their body will look good. It will have a fairly good complexion, and people will not find their body especially repulsive. The eyes will not be gaping wide open but will be half-open. The corpse will probably smell good within limits, and because of the involvement of devas and devis, there could be rainbows in the sky, rains of flowers, and so on. None of this means that the person has achieved enlightenment or liberation. In this case it just means they are headed for a higher rebirth. Meanwhile in the bardo, as the interval being moves toward a deva rebirth, they will see how gods and goddesses are occupied with entertainment and play and they will think, "I want to go there." It is actually their attachment to the activity of the gods that forms the immediate condition for rebirth there. Those who are born as devas do so because of their karma, but the immediate condition that actually propels them into that birthplace is attraction to it.

The second of the higher realms is the realm of the asuras, or jealous gods. Asuras are similar to gods except they are much more violent and aggressive. Therefore the experience of someone who is going to be reborn as an asura is, in general, similar to the experience of someone who is reborn as a deva. Asuras feel prouder and more aggressive. Rather than seeing the entertainment and amusements of the gods, they see asura soldiers putting on armor, taking up sharp weapons, and attacking one another. The warfare of the asuras is fast and constant and violent, like constant lightning. When devas see the god realm they give rise to attachment or desire, but the asuras give rise to a kind of proud anger. They think, "I've got to join in that battle." It is another form of attachment, but it is an attachment that is an attachment to battle and conflict, and that is the immediate condition that propels them into that birth.

The third higher realm is the human realm. Those who are reborn there are attracted to situations and circumstances, such as the prosperity of humans and the pleasures of the human realm. In particular, they are said to witness the union of their future parents. Seeing that gives rise to intense desire for the parent who will be of the opposite sex, along with intense resentment and jealousy of the parent who will be of the same sex. In the human realm it is this combination of desire and aversion that propels them into the birthplace, which in the case of humans is the womb. What happens as a result of this conjoining of desire and aversion is that the consciousness of the interval being dives into the body of the father via one or another of the sense apertures. Then, together with the father's sperm, the consciousness ends up in the ovum of the mother and the womb. It is at that point that a human being is conceived, and its consciousness is locked in.

The first of the lower realms is the animal realm. Animals, in general, are so bewildered that they are reborn through an almost instinctive and very primitive reaction that is also compulsive and compounded of attachment and aversion. Depending upon what type of animal it is, it will have something to do with a womb or an egg, and so on. The animal realm is similar to the human one except that it is much coarser. The emotions are coarser and the bewilderment is stronger.

Pretas, the second of the lower states, are particularly miserable animals. They are low on the evolutionary scale and are a primitive or undeveloped species. They generally do not take birth through attachment, however, interval beings do not look at the preta realm or at the realm of some form of microscopic life, and think, "I really want to go there." That is not the way it works. Again, what drives you into that type of birth is your karma, but the proximate or immediate condition is that you are fleeing something else. You end up choosing that rebirth because there is something that you are so afraid of that you take shelter from it through birth as a preta. You may be fleeing a violently turbulent ocean, or a forest fire, landslide, or earthquake. You may be fleeing the destruction of an entire mountain or the fierce wind that breaks up a planet at the end of time, or you may be running away from the violent cries of terrifying beings at war. You could be seeing various demonic creatures such as yakshas or fierce predatory animals, or you could be driven into the birth by a blizzard.

In short, if you are going to be reborn as a preta or a lower animal, you are fleeing something. You are trying to get as far away as possible, so you naturally flee into something that looks like a close, confining, and dark space. You look for a shelter, such as caves, holes in the earth, hollow tree trunks, holes in walls or buildings, or spaces in between the leaves of thick foliage. In short, you go into a dark, dark space. You are afraid of being out in the open, and it is the attitude of desire for the dark space of shelter in reaction to something you are afraid of that causes you to be reborn as a preta or lower animal.

The third of the lower states are the hell realms. Because there are very many different hell realms, the actual circumstances that propel one towards rebirth in them can vary quite a bit. An example of a proximate or immediate condition for hellish rebirth may be that you see an attractive forest or mountainside with wild animals moving around and with what appear to be hunters stalking them. You will be attracted to the action of hunting and think, "I have to go there. I want to take part in this and kill some, too." That thought will pull you into the situation, but as soon as you are locked into it, the whole scene will change. The hunted animals, and possibly also the hunters, will change into demonic beings, henchpersons of Yama. They will grab hold of you, take you into custody, and pull you down to hell, where they will start doing their stuff—killing you, cutting you up, and doing all the things that happen to you in hell.

Some beings that are born in hell will not even get that far in the bardo, especially if they led particularly bad lives. Even while they are still alive, they may start to see the servants of Yama on their deathbed, and they will die in a state of terror. Such persons, and in general those who are reborn in hell, leave behind bodies that people find unaccountably scary. People just look at the body and feel freaked out. The body will actually look unpleasant; not just scary but unpleasant as well.

Sometimes a dying person who is going to be reborn in hell will lose consciousness before the whole dissolution or shutdown process is completed. They will faint or lose consciousness in reaction to the agony of death and go through the whole dissolution process without being conscious. Then they wake up unaware that they are dead, and of course their first thought is, "Where and what is my body?" In some cases, as soon as they realize that a mental body has been formed, they will realize that this interval body is not like their preceding aggregates. In this particular case, they will perceive that their mental body is a round, globular mass. It is a sphere with one eye on top of it, like a ball with an eye, and it seems to be blown upward by a very fierce wind. It is blown way up, and then the wind stops and it falls down and lands on a surface of red-hot iron. As it lands, it splatters and melts, then re-forms instantly into the horrific body of a hell being.

Hell beings have bodies that are physically sensitive but extremely horrific. As soon as the hell body has been formed, the being is apprehended by the guardians of that particular hell, who start to torture and kill them in various ways. Many, not all, but many of the beings who are reborn in either the hell realms or as pretas seem to experience being captured by the henchpersons of Yamaraja, the Lord of the Dead, and put on trial, where everything they ever did is recounted. They are charged and judged by Yama, then are led into their next rebirth in a state of great terror. This does not happen universally. It does not happen to everyone who is reborn in those realms, but it does appear to happen to some.

Sometimes another proximate condition for rebirth, if you are going to be reborn in a hot hell, is that you start to experience intense cold in the interval. You flee from the intense cold, thinking, "I really want to go to a warm place," and the warmest place your mind can find is the realm in which you are going to take birth. Then you are born there, and it is too warm. On the other hand, if you are going to be reborn in a cold hell, the opposite happens, and you start to experience suffering of intense heat in the interval. You flee that and are reborn in a cold hell. In this way, even in the hell realms, beings are sometimes born through a kind of craving that is produced by rejection of one thing and choosing something else in its stead.

In general, the immediate or proximate conditions for rebirth are based on one of the four types of physical rebirth: instantaneous, moisture and warmth, egg, or womb. The immediate condition for taking birth instantaneously, without physical generation, is attachment to place or location. Species that are produced by heat and moisture are generally beings that are cast into that birth through attachment to scent and taste. Beings that are born in either womb or egg are generally cast into that birth by attachment to the sexual union of their parents that forms the physical condition for that birth. In any case, the various forms of bewilderment and bewildered appearances that arise in the interval cause you to generate attachment for a certain mode of rebirth and therefore to be cast into it. In this way, the wheel of birth after birth keeps on turning, and it never stops because each time we die we again find ourselves compelled to attach to and take a certain type of rebirth. All of these situations describe the experience of the third phase or third part of the interval of possibility.

Next the text focuses on the means by which you can avoid negative rebirths. The first and primary instruction is to rely upon the remedy for whatever type of reaction you would normally have toward that appearance, whatever it is. An appearance may be anything you see or experience in the interval, whether pleasant and attractive or unpleasant and frightening. To rely upon the remedy, of course, you must have tamed your mind. In order to have any resources at this point in the interval, you must have trained yourself in the various remedies for the various types of things and your reactions to those things. Whatever happens or might happen under those circumstances, you must have the necessary ability to keep your mind tamed and in control. The aspiration here is, "May I therefore at that point not be separated from whatever yogic practices I am trained in."

Here, as in the two earlier stages of the interval, what happens to you principally depends upon the degree of your training and the degree of your ability to bring that training along with you into the after-death state. At this point, as before, you will apply whatever is your principal training. Your practice may be Mahamudra or the Great Perfection or the Great Middle Way, or it may be the cultivation of a state of great and impartial compassion—any of these means can be used at this phase in the interval.

There are other particular means that can be helpful as well. These include the four roots or principals among the six dharmas of Naropa. The first is the practice of chandali, which here is called the "self-blazing of bliss and warmth." Second is the practice of illusory body, by which you learn to view all that appears and everything that exists as illusory, thereby bringing about self-liberation of the eight mundane dharmas. Third are the instructions on dream, by which you cause the bewilderment of the dream state to be purified within the dream state itself. Finally, there are the practices concerning the clear light. In general, all forms of bewilderment and ignorance in the waking state, in the state of deep sleep, and so forth can be purified through these specific practices.

You could apply whichever other practice or combination of practices you are trained in. For example, if you have maintained a stable practice of the generation stage, which means the visualization of deities, you would at this point employ both the technique of visualizing yourself as your deity and also the technique of recognizing the forms that appear to you as deities. That is to say, you not only transform appearances as the deity but also are able to recognize other appearances to be deities as they occur. Normally beings in the interval do see actual deities appearing before them, but some of these are wrathful, and all of them, as we saw before, are intimidating in their brilliance. If threatened by these appearances, you will not recognize them as deities, as sources of refuge, and you will flee from them. Someone who is assiduously trained in the generation stage may be able to recognize the deities and also to transform the experience of the interval into the appearance of deities with all of their features— holding scepters and making the sound of mantras, for example.

If you have cultivated devotion in the practice of guru yoga, you would principally practice guru yoga at this point. By visualizing your guru on top of your head and supplicating your guru for rebirth in a pure realm, you could succeed, even in this third phase of the interval, in being reborn in a completely pure realm. This is not because gurus favor those who pray to them over those who do not. Authentic gurus have equal compassion for all beings and are utterly impartial, but a person's devoted supplication is necessary for the guru to lead them to the pure realm. Therefore, at this point in the interval, practitioners of guru yoga would employ this method and could achieve liberation through it.

An important factor here is the moral discipline you have maintained. For example, authentic monastics who have maintained flawless moral discipline in the immediately preceding life can invoke the merit and power of that. The momentum of that merit will counteract the kleshas such as desire and so forth that form the immediate conditions for rebirth. By dedicating the merit of your moral discipline to rebirth in a pure realm, you will be able to achieve it. Yet another faculty that can be evoked at this point, regardless of technique, is the power of intensive mindfulness and alertness. This can be evoked, regardless of its association with one method or another, because at this point you are trying to block the gates to rebirth in any impure realm. What you want to achieve in this third stage of the interval is to avoid samsaric rebirth altogether and be reborn only in a pure realm, and you can do this using any of the particular methods that were just described. If, however, the compulsion of karma is so strong that you cannot stop yourself from being reborn in samsara, then your next resort is to choose a better rather than worse birth. The birth you want to choose is one where you will be able to practice the Vajrayana and proceed toward awakening. Therefore you want to choose to be reborn as a human being possessing the six elements, and specifically a human being who will in your next life have access to and complete the practice of the supreme path of Vajrayana. The aspiration here is, "May I create the excellent interdependent circumstances for the continued practice of this path."

In order to choose an appropriate rebirth, regard your taking birth at this time as an act of conscious emanation. That is to say, you achieve an emanation body in the sense of consciously choosing birth, rather than being born through the force of karmic compulsion described earlier. You do this by aspiring to undertake or accept the type of birth that will be of the most benefit—the most benefit to others and the most benefit for your own completion of the path. You can choose your family, as well as your gender, race, country, social circumstances, and so on—whatever you want, whatever you decide is going to be best. You may choose to be male or female; you may choose to be born in one place or another. The point here is that you have gained the power of choice, and in order to employ this effectively, you need to apply the faculties of mindfulness and alertness throughout the conception, gestation, and birth process. If you can do this, then you will not succumb to the confusion and bewilderment that fetuses normally undergo. The aspiration here is that you maintain mindfulness and alertness during the threefold process of conception, gestation, and birth, through applying the wisdom of the third empowerment. You aspire to achieve a form of birth that will cause you to be happy in your next life and to proceed to further happiness because you will use your life for the practice of the dharma.

Because your aspiration is to take birth in a form that will be most beneficial, you will usually choose birth in a pure realm as your first resort. In that case, you would continue from then on to be reborn in pure realm after pure realm unless there was specific reason to do otherwise. It could be that through compassion you would take rebirth in an impure realm such as this one. In any case, after you have achieved the higher levels, you would produce emanations in both pure and impure realms. In short, your aspiration is that in the long run you be able to accomplish all forms of buddha activity through producing countless emanations in both pure and impure realms.

The text now summarizes everything that has gone before, saying that from now on, you will always aspire to prepare yourself for the interval by thinking, "This is what I will do when this happens. If that happens, I will do this." By consciously engaging your mind in this manner, not merely thinking about it from time to time, you will be prepared.

As soon as excellent interdependent circumstances arise, you will be able to respond to the circumstances appropriately. In that way, the text concludes, "May I train in the transference from one state to another that constitutes the interval."

Training in this way involves the strong inculcation of a highly motivated aspiration. This is true whether you are working with the delusions of the waking state, of the dream state, or of the interval state. For example, in order to train with the dream state, the primary factor is to initially generate a highly motivated aspiration immediately before sleep. The aspiration could be, "I will recognize that I am dreaming, while I am dreaming. Recognizing it, I will not feel fear, no matter what I dream. I will transform the contents of dreams at will. I will change one thing into a hundred (for example, my body into a hundred), and I will change negative things into positive things."

This type of aspiration to recognize the dream state and transform it will give you the ability to do so, because the aspiration itself, if highly motivated, is the primary factor in success. It is the same for the interval. Preparation for the interval consists in large part of learning what will happen, bringing it to mind, and consciously and repeatedly preparing yourself to respond with the appropriate remedy to each stage as it comes up.

Please dedicate the virtue of receiving these instructions, and all virtue accumulated by yourself and others throughout the past, present, and future, to the ability of each and every being to recognize the various experiences of the interval as they occur. Dedicate this merit to the ability of each and every being to respond to these experiences with appropriate mindfulness and alertness, thereby achieving liberation through rebirth in pure realms. Let all of those liberated beings, having achieved liberation, work tirelessly to liberate others until finally all six realms of sentient beings have, without exception, achieved perfect awakening.

QUESTIONS AND ANSWERS

Student: Rinpoche, if we are beginners on the path and may not be capable of having stability of body, speech, and mind training in this way, what can we do to train for the time of death?

Rinpoche: There are several things you can do to prepare for death and the interval after death. These include the accumulation of merit, the purification of obscurations, the cultivation of as much love and compassion for other beings as you can, and also regular contemplation of what will occur in the interval through studying the *Great Liberation Through Hearing in the Bardo*. Prepare yourself by imagining what it is you are going to be going through at that time. This could also involve meditation on the forms of the peaceful and wrathful deities and the repetition of their mantras. That meditation should also include the reinforced recognition that these deities are innate to you, they are part of you. Although they appear outside you in the interval, they are not separate from you. It is especially important to dedicate the merit of whatever dharma practice you do for the rebirth of yourself and all others in Sukhavati, the realm of Amitabha, because this is supreme among all pure buddha realms. It is greatest in its qualities, and it is also easy to achieve rebirth there for anyone who wishes to. In that way you can insure that, even if you are not capable of achieving liberation in the dharmakaya at death, you can achieve liberation in either the sambhogakaya or nirmanakaya.

Student: Rinpoche, you mentioned ejection of consciousness at one point in the dying process. Could you talk more about that—when it is done, what it means?

Rinpoche: The ejection of consciousness refers to the practice through which the emergence of consciousness from the body of the dying person is controlled and directed. Specifically, the consciousness is directed so that it emerges or is ejected out of the aperture at the top of the person's head. The value of this is that, even if the dying person led a rather evil existence, if the consciousness emerges out of the top of the person's head, that person will at the very least be reborn with a precious human body. If they were a dharma practitioner, they will very likely be reborn in a pure realm. There is great significance and advantage to this practice.

In general, the ejection of consciousness can be achieved in two ways. In one way, the dying person does it for him or herself, and in the other somebody else assists them by doing it for them. In order to practice the ejection of consciousness for your own benefit, you need to receive the instructions and then perform the practice assiduously until the signs of having gained this ability have arisen. There are many systems of ejection practice. The most convenient for general use is the system associated with the Amitabha cycle of teachings. When the person has practiced it until they achieve the ability to eject their consciousness, there will be physical signs, specifically itching or other irritation of the aperture at the top of the head and possible eruption or exuding of fluids, such as lymph and blood. Later on, when they are absolutely certain that they are dying, the person can perform the ejection of consciousness and will be able to do so successfully. Exceptions to this are when the dying person, although trained in the ejection of consciousness, has subdued faculties. For example, their mind may be dull because of medication or the illness, or they may be so terrified by death that they forget to do it. Under those circumstances they require the assistance of someone else.

The person who assists by performing the ejection of consciousness for another needs to have practiced it himself or herself until achieving the signs of the ability. Only thereafter will they have the ability to do it for somebody else. In any case, they must perform the ejection of consciousness for the dying person exactly at the critical moment, and it must not be done before then. Ejection of consciousness is of great benefit if it is performed at the right time, especially if the person for whom it is performed is a practitioner. If this person has trained in the ejection of consciousness himself or herself, the benefit will be certain and far greater than the benefit to an ordinary person. It is of the greatest importance that the ejection of consciousness not be performed before the death process is irreversible. If it is performed when there is still hope of resuscitation or survival, then if you do it to yourself it is suicide and if you do it to another person it is murder.

Student: You talk about the consciousness leaving the body, and after that the person in the bardo has ideas and visions of himself as certain things. For example, he sees himself in the body that he used to have and he sees himself in the body that he is going to have. When the consciousness leaves the body, what part of him actually perceives that?

Rinpoche: The person is the consciousness, not the body.

Student: Right now I am caring for someone who is aged, and she's experiencing lots of delusions and demented experiences. When you were describing some of the frightening, fearful experiences in the bardo, it reminded me of some of the things that she has been going through. I was wondering if something of the bardo enters into the dying process, and what Rinpoche could suggest that I could do for her.

Rinpoche: She is not experiencing a phase of the bardo. She is experiencing hallucinations that are caused by the deterioration of the parts of the brain that result in the condition. Because this condition consists of a deterioration of the channels and so forth within the brain, it makes communication with the person, and helping them in a meaningful way, very challenging. It is hard to know exactly what you can do, but she is not experiencing the bardo yet.

Student: Rinpoche, at what point would you know that it is time to eject the consciousness for another person? How can you tell?

Rinpoche: The actual point at which the ejection of consciousness proper should be performed is when the breathing stops, and the usual criterion for this is to observe when the pulse in the neck stops. You can perform the ejection of consciousness after the pulse has ceased. Up to that point, you should prepare for it through the preliminary recitation of the names of buddhas and the various liturgical practices associated with it that prepare the person to receive the guidance.

Student: Why is it that it is more beneficial to eject the consciousness from the upper apertures? What determines that? Why is it the upper ones and not others?

Rinpoche: Ordinarily a person's consciousness never leaves from the upper aperture. It usually leaves out of one of the sense doors or the lower gates. The only circumstances under which someone's consciousness will naturally emerge out of the aperture at the top of the head is if they are someone with extraordinary virtue or merit, or they are someone who has familiarized themselves to some degree with the ejection of consciousness. Otherwise it simply will not go out from there. The reason is that the departure of the consciousness from the body in that direction is the avenue to rebirth in a pure realm. More often than not, a person's consciousness leaves out of the lower parts of their body, and that is almost invariably an indication of a lower rebirth.

Student: My cousin died this past week. She was someone who was close to my family and almost like a sister to us. But she didn't practice any of this, and was not exposed to the dharma. So now she's in the bardo. I asked for a lamp to be lit for her for forty-nine days. How am I helping her or somebody else in the bardo who has no exposure or connection to these teachings?

Rinpoche: In such cases the intervention of someone like you, who has sincere compassion for the deceased, actually helps a person in spite of their previous absence of connection with dharma, especially when you dedicate your virtue and merit to them. There are many instances of this. For example, it is said that if you say the names of buddhas or certain mantras in the ear of an animal recently dead, that will prevent that animal from being born in lower states. Now that animal certainly had no connection with dharma in life, but nevertheless it can be benefited in this way.

Student: What would be appropriate practices when we are with someone at the moment they die? You just suggested that we would recite mantras and names of deities. Are there any other appropriate things we can do at that moment?

Rinpoche: Well, the type of thing you would do would depend basically upon your own degree of knowledge. At the very least you could certainly recite mantras and the names of buddhas and so on. Doing so with an attitude of love and compassion for that person would actually help them. This type of spiritual assistance is the most important thing to do for someone who is dying. Up to that point your primary effort has been to make them comfortable, but they are getting to the point where that is no longer an issue.

Student: Rinpoche, about twelve years ago, I was visiting a friend of mine in the hospital who had AIDS, and he asked me to meditate with him. So I did. I led him in a very brief meditation. I just made something up which would help him relax because I knew that he was very angry that he had AIDS. I didn't think he was going to die right then, but as it turned out, after I meditated with him, he closed his eyes. I stepped away but kept an eye on him, and it probably wasn't even five minutes after that I saw that he was no longer breathing. So I went right over to him. I had heard of the Tibetan Book of the Dead, *but I didn't know enough to say anything so I just whispered to him, "It's okay, don't be afraid, don't be afraid, it's okay, Peter." After I did that for maybe five minutes, they called the nurse in and he was dead. I always felt okay about that, in fact I felt very fortunate that I was right there when he died. For some reason I just felt that way. I never thought I would.*

I'm thinking about this for myself because I'm getting older and my practice is just okay. I'm not a great practitioner, yet the dharma is always on my mind. I do the best I can with that; sometimes I do well and sometimes I don't and I regret it. Now I'm faced with dying myself. I can imagine that if I was doing a good practice, that I could look forward to dying with a certain amount of confidence, that it would be an okay death. And I know that that does happen.

Rinpoche: To answer your first point, the assistance you gave your friend was both altruistic and caring, and therefore it could only have been helpful. Especially your conveyance to him of assurance and the reduction of his fear would actually have helped him in the interval after death.

81

I cannot guarantee that he achieved liberation, but what I can tell you is that by making him less afraid at the beginning of the interval, you created a greater chance for him to do well in the interval.

With regard to your second point, I am a lot older than you are so I've got more to worry about. Therefore this is of great concern to me, too, so I'll tell you what I really think. The single best preparation that you can have for dying is to recite the mantra OM MANI PEME HUNG. If you make the commitment to yourself, "I will recite 100 million OM MANI PEME HUNG's", whether or not you complete it in this life, from the day you make that commitment until the day you die, this will have a great effect on you, and you will have tremendous benefit. As for what you meditate on, you should always visualize above your head either the Buddha Amitabha or the bodhisattva Chenrezik, it does not matter which. Just think that the deity is the embodiment in one form of all sources of refuge and especially of all of your spiritual teachers. Continually visualize them there, above your head, day and night, and resolve that at death your consciousness will dissolve upward into them. What you meditate on and visualize is your teacher in the form of Amitabha or Chenrezik above your head, and what you recite is the mantra OM MANI PEME HUNG. That is the best preparation.

Student: Rinpoche, I'm concerned about the possibility of having impaired mental functions at the time of death due to medication or to illness. What is the best thing to do if this is the case? What if a person's functions are so reduced by a coma that they cannot practice at all at the time of death, let alone for possibly ten or fifteen years before the time of their death? If their mental functions are so incredibly impaired, what is the best thing? Is there any hope for them to improve their situation at the time of death, or are they just left to their karma completely at that point, as if they hadn't practiced at all during that lifetime?

Rinpoche: It is by no means the case that, if you are in a coma or have otherwise impaired faculties at the time of your death, this will wipe out the benefit of your practice previous to that time. As you indicated in your question, because you will not be conscious, it will be very difficult to make immediate use of the practice or what you learn through your practice. If a person who is in a coma or whose faculties are impaired has an attending lama at their death, then the lama will be able to communicate with them. When the shutdown process of dying reaches the point where the person's mind is, although still within the body, no longer biologically seated in it, then their mind becomes independent of the physical conditions that produced the impairment.

Usually a state of coma or unconsciousness, or a state of diminished faculties is produced by physical conditions such as damage to the brain or medications that prevent brain functioning. Once the body has shut down, then the consciousness has an alertness that is independent of these physical conditions, so the person would become conscious at that point, although it would not be physically evident. At that point, the lama could perform the ejection of consciousness, and could also communicate with the person, giving them guidance, and they would be able to understand it.

It is also possible that the person could become conscious at the point where their mind has biologically separated from the body. But you cannot depend on that, because it is also possible that other habits would intervene and the person's previous habits of practice might not reassert themselves. Therefore the dependable resort under those circumstances would be to have an attending lama.

Student: Rinpoche, you mentioned before that the ejection of the consciousness through the crown sometimes manifests with some sort of physical appearance. Is it always the case that when the consciousness ejects through one of the gates of the body a physical manifestation occurs, and how would it occur through some of the other gates or orifices?

Rinpoche: The physical evidence, such as exuding lymph and blood and so on, is not a sign that the consciousness has been ejected. It is a sign that the person has gained the ability to eject it. When the consciousness is actually ejected, either from that gate or from any other, there will be no such swelling or sign.

Student: Rinpoche, some people who are from a different religious orientation have a very strong concept about their religion. I have heard that if you recite the Buddha's mantras that are foreign to them, this would also be very scary for them because they have fears about other religions. How would you work with that?

Rinpoche: Well, what you say is very true. In those situations you have to do whatever you do for their benefit silently, such as cultivating compassion for them and doing silent visualizations or meditations. If you recite the names of buddhas or Buddhist mantras in the hearing of someone who is a staunch adherent of another religious tradition, at the very least they are going to feel disoriented and possibly betrayed. They will think, "They are denying my source of refuge or my savior and trying to appeal to another," and that will anger them. So you have to be silent.

Student: Rinpoche, speaking of my own death, if I am dealing with pain, I understand that it is better to go without medication so I can be clear. When I am dying is it better to try to sit up and maintain a meditative posture? I am also curious about whether to lie on the left or the right side to prepare for death.

Rinpoche: With regard to the use of pain medication, if someone has a strong enough practice such that, by maintaining full clarity of mind during the dying process, they will be able to achieve liberation, then they should avoid any pain medication that will excessively dull their faculties, if possible. Otherwise if their practice is not that strong, it is better that they receive whatever medication will alleviate their suffering. As far as physical posture at the time of death, of course, it is excellent to die sitting up straight, but most people cannot do that because, after all, they are dying. In that case, it is better to lie on the right side in the posture that the Buddha adopted at his death.

Student: When the red and white elements and the life wind withdraw into the heart center, is that an irreversible process or is it something that someone might experience during a near-death experience where the life functions appear to have ceased but are then revived?

Rinpoche: The full process, in which all of the pressure exerted by the life wind is gone and the drops descend and ascend respectively to the heart and combine there, does not happen unless the person has reached the irreversible stage, which is the third stage of attainment. Up until then, there is merely some weakening of the life wind. There could be some movement, but not the full process; that is, only up through the first two stages of dissolution—the white appearance and the red increase. Up to that point it might be reversible—in other words, that does happen in near-death experiences, but the third stage doesn't.

Student: Can you elaborate a little bit more on that, and the stage just prior to when that occurs? When the drops are coming together? You were talking about practicing in this life to recognize the ground clear light when it occurs. If you miss it when it happens, is that the point when you move on to the second part of the interval?

Rinpoche: The preparation in this life for the recognition of the ground clear light does not normally consist of simulating the process of dissolution, but of generating a state of even-placement where the mind is immersed in what is called "the path clear light." This state of even-placement is not necessarily connected with the process of shutdown or dissolution. The border between the first and second parts of the interval of possibility, the whole dying and death process, is the appearance of the ground clear light. The appearance of the ground clear light is the fourth stage of dissolution, the fourth moment. It is the actual moment of death and if it is not recognized, then the person enters what we call the bardo proper.

Student: Regarding the descending and ascending of the life wind in the central channel, I've always thought that the central channel is symmetrically in the center of our physical body. We know that our heart is asymmetrically placed in the body, so when we talk about the heart are we are talking about a place in the central channel at the same level as the physical heart but symmetrically in the center of the body?

Rinpoche: It means the central channel at the height of the heart.

Student: I've heard that forty-nine days is the general amount of time within which the whole process of rebirth takes place, but this is hard to pin down. Technically when do you start counting? Do you start counting from the day the person dies? Secondly, do most of the things that you compared to the dharmakaya, sambhogakaya, and nirmanakaya generally happen right away in that period of forty-nine days?

Rinpoche: To answer your first question, or perhaps to further obscure it, there are two systems for reckoning the forty-nine-day period. One system is that if you die today, the first day starts with sunrise tomorrow. The other way is based on the fact that people are only sporadically conscious for the first three days after death in the bardo. That system discounts the first three days and starts on the fourth sunrise after death. If you start at sunrise tomorrow, you can call the first days "A, B, and C," and then count the next day as the first of the forty-nine days.

These are not so much different opinions about how the period should be counted as different ways they can be applied depending upon what happens to the individual. Assuming that there is no recognition of the ground clear light, some people become unconscious but stay in the body. They will remain unconscious for two or three days, and then their consciousness will leave the body. For those people, it is better to reckon it with the three days excluded.

Other people with slightly different channels, who also do not recognize the ground clear light, leave their body as soon as the ground clear light has passed. For those people it is obviously better to start counting the morning of the next day. The problem is that there is no obvious way to tell which is happening, because although there are signs of someone recognizing the ground clear light, as described earlier, there are no really obvious signs of whether the person's consciousness has remained or left after failing to recognize it. Basically, then, one or another of the two customs will be applied more or less arbitrarily.

As for the correlation between the forty-nine-day period and the opportunities of the three kayas, the opportunity to achieve liberation in the dharmakaya is the ground clear light. If someone recognizes it, then they will remain immersed in it for the period of their ensuing samadhi, which is normally three days but can be longer. They are in a totally different category, because they are not in the bardo. For someone in the bardo who does not recognize the clear light, the dharmakaya window of opportunity is gone as soon as they do not recognize it, because the ground clear light will cease, and they will move on to the next part, which is the *opportunity to achieve the sambhogakaya*.

The sambhogakaya window is twofold, and in most Kagyu presentations the two aspects are not classified sequentially, as in "window one" and "window two." Obviously "window" here is not literal, but I think it is the best word. The first aspect of the opportunity for liberation in the sambhogakaya is the *appearances of spontaneous presence*, which means the rays of wisdom light and the peaceful and wrathful deities. According to the *Great Liberation Through Hearing in the Bardo*, this goes on for several days, and in that book you will see an exact schedule for what happens on each day. These appearances last for a couple of weeks, and there is a progressive coarsening and therefore a greater difficulty of liberation. At the same time, there is the opportunity for another type of liberation. In this second aspect of the sambhogakaya window, the practitioner is able to cause their mental body to arise in the form of a deity, in which case they achieve liberation in the form of that deity. In the Kagyu tradition, we classify both of these opportunities as sambhogakaya windows, but we do not consider that first one happens and then the other. The opportunities for either are more or less simultaneous.

The opportunity for the achievement of nirmanakaya begins when you are approaching rebirth, and your principal effort is to stop an undesirable rebirth and instead choose your rebirth. Calculating exactly how long this period lasts brings up the whole issue of the forty-nine-day period as a whole. The forty-nine-day period is considered an average time or duration of the interval—the whole thing—but it is by no means certain that any specific individual will remain in the interval for that long or for only that long. Generally speaking, the stronger your karma in one direction or another, good or bad, the more quickly you are likely to achieve rebirth. To the extent that you have cultivated extraordinary virtue, there will be almost immediate rebirth in a pure realm. If you cultivated great evil, there could be almost immediate rebirth in a lower realm.

If someone's balance of wrongdoing and virtue is pretty well even, the karmic propulsion will be less focused, causing their rebirth to be less certain, and they might remain in the interval for even longer than forty-nine days. In any case, the nirmanakaya opportunity is over when the person either successfully or unsuccessfully enters their next place of birth. "Successfully" means that they have used this period of the interval to achieve the nirmanakaya; in other words, through the forces of aspirations, moral discipline, love, and compassion they have consciously chosen a rebirth that will be of benefit to themselves and others. That is what achievement of the nirmanakaya means in this particular context. "Unsuccessful" means uncontrolled rebirth. In either case, that is when it ends.

Student: Rinpoche, from what you said earlier, I have the impression that your rebirth is determined largely by the choices you make in the interval state, when you see the five lights of wisdom and the five lights of samsaric rebirth. I always heard that it was your karma that determines your rebirth, so how do you reconcile this? Is it your karma that propels you to make one choice over another?

Rinpoche: That question brings up the primary significance of the interval. Birth is the full ripening of karma; in other words, when you are conceived and you enter the place of birth, you become locked into the results of previous actions. Once you have a certain birth, your actions have ripened as the aggregates of a certain life, and there's not much you can do about it. You cannot change it all of a sudden. It may change through adventitious circumstances, but basically, for as long as you remain alive in that life, you are limited by those circumstances and you have no choice about it.

What happens when you die is that the karma that propelled you into a certain life and allowed you to take a certain rebirth has been used up. There remain some habits of your previous life, as is evidenced, for example, by perceiving yourself in your previous body and so on. Nevertheless the actual karma is gone, and the karma that will cause your next rebirth has not yet taken effect. Because you have several different such karmas within your being, it may not yet be certain which rebirth you are going to take.

In a sense, when you are in the interval between lives, you are in a gap that is in between karmically locked circumstances. While you are in between, you can, if you know how to do so, make some changes and some choices. You cannot do this once you have entered the place of birth and are locked into the next life. That is why the power of a virtuous state of mind in the interval is tremendous. It can actually bring an immediate and great change to what happens to you.

Student: Rinpoche, what can you do when someone dies? I'm thinking of my parents. How do I stay calm enough to do practice? I'm afraid I'll be too upset to be effective. I thought of going on a retreat after one of them dies to do practice. Is it a good idea to go on retreat for someone? How long should the retreat be, and which practice should you do?

Rinpoche: Of course, the state of sadness or grief that results from the death of people we love happens to us. The best thing you can do when you are going through this is to reflect upon the fact that death is natural. Everyone dies, at some point everyone is going to die and is not going to be here anymore. In that way, you acknowledge that parting and separation from those you love is simply a fact of life. Continuing in that way of thinking, you should reflect upon the fact that you too are going to die, exactly like those for whom you are grieving. By thinking in those terms, you transform the potentially paralyzing grief into a source of inspiration, because the best opportunity for someone to practice is when some event such as the death of one of their parents has brought impermanence vividly before their mind. So you should think, "If I cannot practice now, I'll be wasting the best possible opportunity."

Student: Rinpoche, can you explain about the death of a young infant or child. How does this work for them? It appears their life has just begun, and they haven't been exposed to practice. What can you do for them?

Rinpoche: All you can do is to recite mantras such as OM MANI PEME HUNG for their benefit and in their hearing, or dedicate all other virtues you perform to their benefit. If you can, perform the ejection of consciousness for them. You cannot really do much more than that.

Student: Rinpoche, you referred earlier to meditating on the clear light, and I'm not sure what that is. Could you explain that? Also, I have been told often to accept impermanence. I think that in Tibetan culture there is much more comfort and practice in working with this, but in our culture we haven't been able to talk about death, except for maybe the last ten years. Many soldiers are dying, and a lot of our friends are dying at a much earlier age because of illness. Perhaps we need to pay much more attention to this. There is a certain freedom in being comfortable with the idea that death is natural, yet I don't think we are all in that place. Could you speak about that?

Rinpoche: To answer your second question first, it is true, as you say, that generally speaking, people live in denial of death. We flee the concept and we are intensely uncomfortable with it. But being uncomfortable with it is actually the starting point of contemplation. Whether you are Tibetan, American, or anything else, if you become comfortable with the idea of death, you may think, "Well, death is coming, impermanence is natural, and that's okay." Simply thinking that death is okay and being comfortable with it does no good whatsoever.

The purpose of the contemplation of death is not to alleviate anxiety about it but to use the approach of death as inspiration for practice. Contemplating death and impermanence causes you to realize that you have no time to waste. It is only if this causes you to practice assiduously that such contemplation has any value or has achieved its intended purpose. The instruction that you have heard and read—to contemplate death and impermanence—really means to take these things to heart so that you are inspired to practice with diligence.

With regard to the contemplation of impermanence, some people seem to have the idea that thinking about death and impermanence all the time will shorten your life, or that you will attract death by thinking about it. This is nonsense. The length of your life is primarily a matter of your karma, and you do not change your karma by thinking about death. If it were true that you shortened your life by thinking about death, then you could lengthen your life endlessly by repeatedly contemplating immortality, and we've seen that that does not happen! Therefore you can reasonably assume that you are in no danger of dying sooner merely because you contemplate impermanence.

As for what constitutes meditation on the clear light, I'll give you an example of it. When you are meditating upon Chenrezik, as I instructed you earlier, you recite the mantra OM MANI PEME HUNG continuously. While reciting the mantra, from time to time rest your mind in a state free of any mental engagement, of any thought or mental activity, and that will be an encounter with the clear light.

Student: I have a question about life releasing. In Boston the earthworms come from Canada. If you buy them, you are creating the karmic preconditions for more earthworms to be scooped up by hardworking Canadians in the north, who pick them up as a sort of cottage industry. Therefore, when you go to release these lives, you are actually putting more lives in jeopardy. Similarly, if you buy baitfish, you are creating a market for more baitfish. I can see how this works very well in a more traditional agrarian economy, but in a capitalist economy, by buying the earthworms or the fish I'm putting more lives in danger. How do I best effect the wish for life release?

Rinpoche: Well, we cannot protect all beings. We have to protect the ones to which we have access, but even those we cannot protect forever. We may only be able to lengthen their lives by as much as one day. So when you buy animals that are being sold for purposes that will involve their death, whether it is their consumption as is the case with fish that are sold live or their use as bait, as is the case with earthworms, even if they only survive for one day, that is probably one day longer than they would have survived otherwise.

Student: In the bardo teachings, the precondition to being able to do anything successfully in this experience is to develop a very strong meditative stability in this life. This is a persistent problem in my practice. I read a lot because I have a very hard time getting any kind of stability in my meditation. Is there any further assistance that will get this to work better?

Rinpoche: There are definitely means and instructions that will enable you to develop the type of stability that is needed to successfully traverse the interval. As you indicated in your question, we all want to achieve this kind of stability. It is not necessarily achieved by practicing a large variety of techniques, but by properly implementing any one complete technique of practice. Visualizing your body as the deity Chenrezik, repeating the mantra OM MANI PEME HUNG, and dissolving the appearance of the deity into emptiness at the conclusion of the session are three techniques by which you can achieve the necessary stability for traversing the interval. The phase of the meditation where you withdraw or dissolve the appearance of the deity is how to cultivate familiarity with the clear light so that you can recognize the dharmakaya at death. Meditating upon your body as the body of Chenrezik is how you can gain the ability to achieve liberation as the sambhogakaya in the second phase of the interval. Repetition of the mantra OM MANI PEME HUNG is how you can learn to view all sound, including the sounds that appear in the interval, as mantra. Furthermore, the motivation of great compassion with which you perform the whole practice is the basis for the altruistic aspiration to be reborn as nirmanakaya for the benefit of others, which is the key to traversing the third phase of the interval, and doing this one complete technique will achieve all that you need. In contrast, knowledge of a large number of techniques without gaining stability in any one of them will not bring this.

Student: Rinpoche, I've been a Buddhist for about 25 years, and I've never tried very hard to avoid eating meat, but it seems that maybe I should do that since we do live in an environment where it is possible to eat a fairly healthy, nutritious diet that excludes meat, unlike other Buddhist environments where it wasn't so easy to do that. Do you recommend that I should be making more of an effort to develop a diet that excludes meat?

Secondly, a lot of us have been reading about these horrible meat factories where much of our meat comes from now, and where the conditions for the animals are even more horrendous than they would be on a regular farm. If we are going to eat meat, should we be trying to make sure that the meat that we are eating does not come from these terrible places?

Rinpoche: If you can stop eating meat, that would be wondrous, and I would thank you and rejoice in your doing so. It is, for all of the reasons you mentioned, obviously better not to eat meat. If you cannot stop eating meat entirely, or if you find yourself traveling to countries where you more or less have to eat meat, then when you eat it, you should use the opportunity to make aspirations that the animal not be reborn in lower states. Because you are making a physical connection with the animal by consuming its flesh and absorbing it into your body, you can actually help the animal by doing this. I am not saying that that makes eating meat okay or that because you make these aspirations, there is no sin in eating meat. There is. It is very hard for me to say this because I have been unable to abandon the consumption of meat myself, so I am not comfortable going around telling people not to eat meat, but if I am asked directly if it is better not to eat meat, I have to say "yes."

Student: My understanding is that if someone recognizes the clear light at the time of death, they achieve the dharmakaya, absolute buddhahood. Now if somebody in their lifetime, as we are now, takes the bodhisattva vow, which is vowing to return in physical form until all beings have achieved liberation, would that somehow be breaking their vow by achieving the dharmakaya state?

Rinpoche: No, it is not a violation of the vow, because when

97

someone achieves the dharmakaya, they do not abide in a passive state or a state without activity. It is not like some sort of permanent vacation. As soon as someone attains the dharmakaya, they automatically display the sambhogakaya and, by extension, the nirmanakaya for the benefit of others. Rather than contravening the bodhisattva vow, it is in fact the most perfect fulfillment of it.

Student: Rinpoche, what kind of things can an individual practitioner do on the anniversary of someone who died? If the person will have already taken rebirth, is it still beneficial for them?

Rinpoche: You can still benefit the person at any time, including the yearly observance of their passing, regardless of whether or not they have been reborn and really regardless of how long it has been since they were reborn. You can benefit them by doing meritorious things such as making offerings dedicated to them or in their name, and by dedicating the virtue of your usual virtuous activities especially to them at that time. In either case, you will be helping yourself and also helping the other person. Even if they have taken rebirth by that time, you do not necessarily know what type of rebirth. If they have taken an unfortunate rebirth, you might be able to ameliorate their circumstances or even free them from that birth by doing virtue for their benefit.

It was not uncommon in Tibet for great lamas to be able to see where deceased people had been reborn. They would sometimes—usually at the request of family members—determine this, and then advise the family on what needed to be done. They would say something like, "Your relative has been reborn in such-and-such lower state. In order to free them from this, the families should perform such-and-such practices, such-and-such virtuous endeavors, and so on." Another event that occurred throughout much of Tibetan history, and still can happen nowadays, is people becoming "returners." Returners are people who actually die and come back. It is more than a near-death experience, because they have actually gone through the whole death process, including the bardo, and they are able, especially if they do this repeatedly, to see lower states and to contact people who have passed away. Even if it has been years since someone has died and been reborn in a lower state, they will sometimes carry messages from that person back to family, advising the family about what needs to be done for their benefit and so on, and this seems to be indeed effective.

Student: There are some people who are on life support for a long time, and there is no chance for them to recover. There is no longer any will left in such a person. What should one do in that situation to end this suffering, when there is no living will and there are obstructions to allowing for a natural death to take place?

Rinpoche: It is hard for me to answer this because the actual effect of artificial life support or resuscitation in most people in the long run is hard to determine. What I can say is that if the person is a strong practitioner who has the chance to recognize the ground clear light at death, then it would be much better that they not be artificially resuscitated. Their life should not be artificially prolonged by life support mechanisms, because these things would prevent them from experiencing the ground clear light while they were still conscious and able to recognize it. When they did eventually enter the clear light, they would be entering it from a state of unconsciousness, which would put them at a disadvantage.

This is not really an issue with an ordinary person because most people do not have a significant chance of recognizing the ground clear light. In that case, whether they enter it through a natural, conscious death or from a state of prolonged unconsciousness is largely irrelevant, because in either case they are simply not going to recognize it. For an ordinary person, it is hard to say whether or not artificial resuscitation and life support actually would do them any harm—it may or may not. To give you an idea of someone for whom it was an issue, the late Lama Ganga, a year before he passed away, said to me, "If I have merit, I will die in Tibet. If I cannot manage that, I'm going to make sure that I die in India. I don't dare to die in America, because they won't let me die. They would hook me up to those machines, and I would not be able to die." Now I interpret his remarks as an indirect expression of his confidence in his ability to recognize the ground clear light and achieve liberation in the bardo, and that is why it was an issue for him.

Student: I heard stories of people who are dying and talking to their relatives who were already dead for some time—it seemed as if they saw the deceaced relatives or heard them. Would talking with deceased relatives and having their presence be helpful in our process of dying?

Rinpoche: I think that they are not actually seeing their relatives—that it is a hallucination produced by the habit of association with those people. You could actually contact dead people only when you yourself are dead, when the shutdown or dissolution process is completed. If the dying person is still talking, then they are not dead yet. They are probably having an appearance or hallucination through habit.

Student: What about people who are from different denominations, who have a different kind of faith or different beliefs? What is the chance of their liberation, and what can be done for them in order to help them with this process?

Rinpoche: With regard to your first question, I really do not know how to answer it. If I were to answer by saying, "No, non-Buddhists have no chance for recognition and liberation," that would be no more than sectarian prejudice on my part. On the other hand, if I were to say, "Yes, they have chance for recognition and liberation," that would be sheer pretentiousness, because to make that statement I would have had to have achieved the final result of their religion and know what abilities it bestowed. So I cannot answer that question.

With regard to your second question, I think you would employ the same methods that you would use for a Buddhist, except you would do it discreetly. For example, you could recite mantras or Buddhist names, such as OM MANI PEME HUNG, and dedicate the merit of that to the person, but you just wouldn't do it so that they heard it, because that would disturb them, as we discussed before. These activities are beneficial to anyone, not just to Buddhists. If you do something virtuous, such as reciting that mantra and dedicating your merit to that person, the fact that they themselves are not Buddhists does not in any way prevent them from benefiting from it. The purpose of dharma is to benefit all beings of the six realms, not merely Buddhists.

Student: Rinpoche, you spoke about karma being used up in the interval, and I wonder if you can elaborate more about karma and how we carry it forward into subsequent lives.

Rinpoche: Karma abides within the all-basis consciousness of an individual, and in the case of the interval it is this all-basis consciousness combined with the subtle wind, the life wind, that goes from life to life. So that wind-mind serves as the container for the maintenance and transportation of karma. I need to make something clear. When I said that the karma of the previous life was used up, I did not mean that all of the accumulated karma that had led to the previous life was used up. I meant that the particular karma, the particular imprint of action, that led to that particular birth must be used up when that birth is finished. This does not mean that all of the other karmic imprints that are stored within the all-basis consciousness have been wiped out or used up. They are all there.

The gap that is experienced in the interval consists of the fact that, while the karmas are still present within your being, the ripening of karma is temporarily dormant. It is a karmically ripened situation, a time when the set of aggregates that have karmically ripened during your life are not present. Karma from the previous life has been destroyed and used up, whereas the karma for the next one is present but has not ripened yet. This makes for a situation where changes can be affected, since what prevents change is the limitation imposed upon you by fully ripened karma. In other words, once a karma has fully ripened or matured resulting in the aggregates of a new life, not much can be done about it. You are stuck in that situation. But in between lives, although you have plenty of karma that needs to be purified, none of it is in a ripened state yet, so changes can be effected.

Student: Rinpoche, how can we as ordinary practitioners, myself or others, benefit beings in the six realms by emptying the lower realms? I'm alluding to liturgies where prayers such as "May the lower realms be emptied" are found. For an ordinary level practitioner, this seems somewhat hard to grasp. When this is our aspiration, how do we begin?

Rinpoche: Even though we are ordinary sentient beings, there is a great deal that we can do for others. Every time that you do something virtuous and sincerely dedicate that virtue to others, you can—through the force of your merit and dedication—introduce virtuous habit into the continuum of other beings. The virtuous habit that is introduced by the strength of your dedication and aspiration will eventually cause them to achieve liberation, first of all from lower states and eventually from cyclic existence itself.

The phrases commonly used in our liturgies, "Emptying samsara from its depths," "Emptying lower states from their depths," and so on, refer to the principal aim and aspiration of all buddhas and bodhisattvas in their compassion, and indeed of all who take the bodhisattva vow. You aspire to bring all beings without exception to liberation. This is an open-ended aspiration in the sense that beings are limit-less, so it is difficult even to answer the question that is often posed, "Will there ever come a time when all beings have been liberated?" This remains what has been called a "difficult point." Although we undertake the aspiration to bring all beings without exception to liberation, and although this is open-ended and possibly an infinite endeav-or, we still can, one-by-one, benefit beings.

There are plenty of situations where, even as an ordinary and afflicted being yourself, you can plant the seed of liber-ation in the being of another. For example, if you say the mantra OM MANI PEME HUNG in the hearing of an animal that has died, you plant the seed of liberation in that being. Anyone who is connected with the Buddha's teaching can do this. It does not require a state of attainment; you sim-ply have to know that it can be done and do it.

As I have said before, I cannot assess whether adherents of other religions can or cannot attain liberation, because I just do not know. What I can say is that those who have no connection to any spiritual tradition whatsoever cannot do it because they have no means at their disposal to introduce the seed of liberation in another's being. We would call those persons truly "ordinary" in the fullest sense of the term. We are also unattained beings, but nevertheless we have knowledge with which we can benefit others. Although we too are ordinary beings, we are the best among the ordinary because we have the means at our dis-posal to benefit others.

Student: In the U.S. we tend to have pets "put to sleep" when they are in their last days and they are suffering a lot.

How do you view this?

Rinpoche: I do not think it is a very good thing, although it is true that animals can suffer tremendously when they are dying, and people do wish to end their suffering. It is much better to attend and assist the animal during its dying process as much as you can, and to allow the animal to die naturally rather than hastening its death by giving it poison. People's motivation in doing this, of course, is compassionate; they do it because they think that experience ceases with death, and that the remaining experience of the animal is just going to be misery and suffering. They naturally want to spare the animal that suffering. Although their motivation is compassionate, it is based on a fundamental misunderstanding, which is the idea that experience ends with death.

The problem with euthanasia is that it often will precipitate a greater experience of suffering that ensues after the animal has died. You may not recognize that because you cannot see it when the animal no longer inhabits its body, but for this reason it is better if you can allow the animal to die naturally.

Student: Rinpoche, when in this process can a near-death experience happen, and when it does, what is happening to the life wind? Also, I've read that in near-death experiences people often say that they see a beautiful, wonderful light and are drawn to it. But it seems that here we are saying that either we do not recognize it, or it would be so bright that we would be fearful of it and shun it.

Rinpoche: It seems that the most common near-death experience is an experience of either appearance or increase. If that is the case, then the person has not yet reached the stage of attainment, which is the stage when there is complete shutdown. Therefore they are not at the point where the truly brilliant and threatening lights appear. They are experiencing the whiteness or the redness, and because this involves the shutdown of certain kinds of conceptuality, it is experienced as pleasant. The power of the life wind is not entirely used up, otherwise the person would not return to life.

Student: Rinpoche, in the context of being reborn in a modern, scientific process such as artificial insemination or conception in a petri dish in a lab, how does this take place? In other words, what takes the place of observing the union of the parents and what becomes the immediate condition? What makes the consciousness dive into the petri dish? What are the mechanics of that?

Rinpoche: It basically works the same way, just as it works the same way physically. The consciousness still identifies the substances, the ovum and the sperm, with the same kleshas. The kleshas are not only directed at individuals, they are directed at the substances themselves, through attraction and repulsion. It is still the same kleshas that cause the consciousness to dive in. Do not forget that the scientific understanding of artificial insemination does not include anything about the way the interval being enters, because they cannot see it.

Student: I'm confused about the dissolution of the two

drops, the two distinct things at the beginning. Is it that the life wind and consciousness, the all-basis consciousness, go into the sperm whether it is in a petri dish or a man's body?

Rinpoche: Yes.

Student: If a being recognizes the dharmakaya, what is their next step? Would they then be capable of choosing a rebirth in a conscious way? Related to that, how would a tulku go through the bardo?

Rinpoche: To answer your first question, if someone recognizes the ground clear light, they achieve the dharmakaya, and at that point they do what any other buddha does. They just engage in boundless activity through the emanation of various form bodies from that point onward until samsara is over. To answer your second question, when a nirmanakaya passes from one life to the next, they basically can do it any way they want to. What they want will depend on what is going to be of the most benefit to the most beings. Obviously, they are not required to pass through a conventional bardo. They may decide to visit the interval in order to benefit and, if possible, liberate other beings in the interval. There are many stories of nirmanakayas who, during their in-between lives, liberate countless beings in the interval. Although they could go to or appear in the interval, visiting lower states and liberating beings there, they would not experience it as a state of compulsion nor one of fear or anxiety.

Student: Rinpoche, how can we use the daily process of falling asleep to help prepare for the process of death? I've heard that during the falling-asleep process you go through some of the same dissolution and clear light experiences. How can we use this? Will you elaborate a little more on what exactly occurs when we fall asleep?

Rinpoche: There is a definite connection between the process of going to sleep and the process of dissolution at death, and this is one of the reasons for the practice of conscious or lucid dreaming, which is how you develop the ability for this recognition.

Student: Rinpoche, your teachings about the interval of possibility have shown me how the practices of Mahamudra and visualization, for instance, relate to the interval between birth and death. Of course, we know the stories of great lamas who achieved liberation during their ordinary lives, like Naropa and Milarepa. The practices described here are aimed at a better chance of achieving liberation during the interval of opportunity. Are the opportunities in ordinary life still so considerable that it is worth aiming for those?

Rinpoche: As you mentioned in your question, individuals like Naropa, Milarepa, and many others achieved perfect awakening in this very life, before death and before encountering anything like the interval. You have the opportunity to do this and to achieve the same thing in this life. In terms of external resources, you have the same dharma that they have, you receive the same instructions they that received, and this dharma and these instructions exist through their kindness. So from the point of view of external resources you have the opportunity.

The problem is that in general we do not have the same

diligence that they had. We do not have the same discernment that they had, or the same faith and devotion. If you cultivate the same diligence, the same discernment, and the same faith and devotion that they had, then you can and will achieve the same thing they achieved. In that sense you do have the opportunity.

In general there are said to be three results of Vajrayana practice. The best result is to achieve perfect awakening, buddhahood, in this very life; the second best result is to achieve it at death or in the interval, and that is what we've been talking about. Thirdly, you can at least achieve liberation quickly in a succession of seven or at the most sixteen lifetimes. This result is the purpose of the practice where you take conscious birth through aspiration in a situation where you will be able to continue Vajrayana practice. The idea is that through further lifetimes you improve, life after life, until you have completed the whole journey.

The point I am making is that even if you do not achieve buddhahood in this lifetime, you are still in the very best of situations, because you are immersed in a system of teaching unique among all Buddhist vehicles, which can lead to awakening so quickly. This teaching is unique to Buddha Shakyamuni, the historical buddha. Basically, no buddha of the past has taught this and no buddha of the future will. We are very fortunate to have access to teachings that even within Buddhist traditions in the more long-term sense are unique.

Student: Rinpoche, do I understand correctly that when you are reborn in the human realm, you are able to see your parents before you take rebirth?

Rinpoche: Yes, you see your parents and that is why you generate the kleshas—the attachment and aversion—that cause the birth.

Student: I've heard it said that you can see a few years into your next life. Is that true?

Rinpoche: In the sense that you already are acquiring a mental body that has the appearance of your future physical body, that would give you some idea. I do not know how precise it is, and I do not know if that means you would actually have conscious knowledge, thinking, "I'm going to be so-and-so, the child of so-and-so and so-and-so."

Student: Rinpoche, since I was a child I've had an interesting connection with reality. At times I have some sense of emptiness, a lasting sense, and as I've developed my practice that has increased somewhat. I think that I've reached a kind of plateau regarding that. At the same time I have a very active dream life, which is occasionally lucid, and I have gained some insight from that as well. However, I have a great deal of difficulty with visualization practice. It would seem that having lucid dreaming and a sense of emptiness, I would be able to have some connection with visualization practice. I feel almost blind. I have a sense of it, but it is not visual. I wonder what I'm experiencing. Am I somehow deluding myself or misapprehending what I am experiencing as emptiness? How I can increase my success with visualization practice?

Rinpoche: Since you have at least a sporadic ability of lucid dreaming, you should try the following: In a lucid dream, go to a cliff or precipice, or confront something that would normally terrify you, like a predator of some kind. See if these disturb you or if the knowledge that you are dreaming prevents you in any way from being afraid of these things. Then try encountering something that you really like or would enjoy, and see if the encounter with something that you are attached to produces any kind of disturbance in your mind. If it does not, if the lucidity of the dream state causes you to be unaffected by frightening or pleasant images, then that is really good.

With regard to your experience of emptiness, it is very difficult to know simply through your mentioning it exactly what it is or what is going on. It could be that you have had spontaneous experiences of your mind in a state of what is called "natural rest," where your mind simply comes to a state of unfabricated rest. If that is what you have been experiencing, then you should be able to apply that easily to visualization practice. To do so, you would start with a fundament of visualization, such as the syllable HRIH. Generate a clear appearance of that alone, transferring the state of natural rest with which you are already familiar to the mental focus on the syllable. You should be able to generate a clear appearance of that syllable, and then gradually extend it to more elaborate visualizations. If that is not what is going on, you may be experiencing a mere absence of mental content which sometimes people experience as a kind of voidness. If it is a mere absence of mental content, then it is of no use whatsoever. It will not help visualization or anything else but is just a mental phenomenon like any other.

With regard to the generation stage in general, we all

want clear visualization, and of course, it is excellent if your visualization is clear. There's nothing wrong with that, but the most important factor is not the actual clarity of the deity that you are attempting to visualize, successfully or unsuccessfully. If the form is insubstantial, with the colorful vividness of a rainbow, and if you can recognize it, then even if the image is extremely vague, the practice is successful, because the main point of it is being practiced. The insubstantial vividness of the image is more important than the degree of clarity. It is quite possible that someone might have the technical ability to generate an extremely clear image, but see it as substantial. Under those circumstances, that would be unsuccessful practice of the generation stage.

Please recite the dedication and aspiration with the wish that through the virtue of this session all beings, having received authentic instructions from eminent teachers, come to recognize the clear light at the time of death and achieve the state of omniscient liberation.

Glossary

AGGREGATES (Skt. skandha) [Tib. phung po] The five phenomenal or psycho-physical constituents that comprise an individual being's experience. They are the aggregate of form (Skt. rupaskandha) [Tib. gzugs kyi phung po], the aggregate of feelings (Skt. vedanaskandha) [Tib. tshor ba'i phung po], the aggregate of perception (Skt. samjnaskandha) [Tib. 'du shes kyi phung po], the aggregate of motivational tendencies or mental formations (Skt. samskaraskandha) [Tib. 'du byed kyi phung po], and the aggregate of consciousness (Skt. vijnanaskandha) [Tib. rnam par shes pa'i phung po].

ALL-BASIS CONSCIOUSNESS (Skt. alayavijnana) [Tib. kun gzhi rnam par shes pa] Of the eight classes of consciousness (Tib. rnam shes tshogs brgyad) according to the yogachara abhidharma, this is the undifferentiated, primordial continuum which underlies the other seven types of consciousness. The all-basis, sometimes known as the "storehouse consciousness," is the repository for all previously accumulated karmic imprints and habitual tendencies.

APPEARANCE STAGE See APPEARANCE, INCREASE, AND ATTAINMENT.

ATTAINMENT STAGE See APPEARANCE, INCREASE, AND ATTAINMENT.

APPEARANCE, INCREASE, AND ATTAINMENT (Tib. snang mched thob gsum) In the first phase of the interval, this threefold

113

shutdown process or subtle dissolution normally occurs when the outer breath has stopped but the inner winds have not yet ceased. This sequence follows the coarse dissolution of the elements and precedes the direct experience of the ground clear light. Each part of this threefold shutdown is also distinguished by three aspects: an appearance, an accompanying cognitive aspect, and a temporary suppression or dormancy of kleshas.

ASPIRATION FOR THE BARDO (Tib. bar do'i smon lam) An aspiration liturgy for liberation in the interval, composed in verse by Chökyi Wangchuk (1584-c.1635), and found in the communal liturgy *Dharma Practices of the Karma Kagyu* (Tib. kam tshang chos spyod).

AVADHUTI (Skt.) [Tib. dbu ma, kun 'dar ma] The central one of three main energy channels in the subtle body.

BARDO See INTERVAL.

CHANDALI (Skt.) [Tib. gtummo] Inner heat yoga. One of the six dharmas of Naropa, made famous by Milarepa. Besides the physical effects of generating heat and bliss, it is a powerful means to bring about realization and complete enlightenment.

CHILD CLEAR LIGHT See under CLEAR LIGHT.

CHILD LUMINOSITY See under CLEAR LIGHT.

CLEAR LIGHT (Skt. prabhasvara) [Tib. 'od gsal] Also translated as "luminosity," the essential nature of mind on the subtlest level, which can be considered synonymous with buddha nature (Skt. sugatagarbha) [Tib. bde gshegs snying po]. Although ever-present within the continuum of every sentient being, it is normally obscured and thus, ordinarily experienced only after the dissolution of the elements and the threefold shutdown processes are completed at the time of death. Recognition of the clear light can, however, be cultivated through familiarization by a practitioner who has trained accordingly. Full recognition thereof is considered attainment of realization of the dharmakaya.

With regard to the clear light, a further distinction is made between two aspects. The first, the ground clear light (Tib. gzhi'i 'od gsal) or mother clear light (Tib. 'od gsal ma), is the aforementioned presence of the dharmakaya that naturally appears at the moment of death, but that cannot be recognized by an ordinary being without sufficient prior familiarization. The second, the path clear light (Tib. lam gyi 'od gsal) or child clear light (Tib. 'od gsal bu), refers to that process of familiarization whereby the practitioner cultivates realization of this essential nature through meditative experience in life. When these two aspects conjoin completely, this is known as the "meeting of mother and child clear lights," and is equivalent to the attainment of perfect awakening or buddhahood.

DHARMAKAYA (Skt.) [Tib. chos kyi sku] The body of truth or reality refers to the noncomposite, nondual, primordially pure essential nature of the awakened mind itself. It is beyond all defilements, afflictions, or conceptual limitations, and is completely clear and unimpeded in its manifestation. The first phase of the bardo is considered to be a prime opportunity to achieve liberation through direct recognition of the dharmakaya.

DHARMATA (Skt.) [Tib. chos nyid] According to the Mahayana, this is the ultimate nature of reality itself, the inexpressible and fundamentally perfect purity of all phenomena.

DREAM YOGA (Tib. rmi lam) [Skt. svapna] One of the six dharmas of Naropa, these advanced yogic meditation practices are primarily aimed at utilizing the dream state as a means to recognize the illusory nature of all appearances, especially as preparation for the interval experience. These techniques involve training in maintaining lucid awareness within the dream state, and actively manipulating the events encountered in dreams.

EIGHT MUNDANE DHARMAS (Skt. astau lokadharmah) [Tib. 'jig rten gyi chos brgyad] Also known as the eight worldly concerns, these are four pairs of opposites: gain and loss, fame and disgrace, praise and criticism, pleasure and pain.

ELEMENTS (Skt. bhuta, dhatu) [Tib. 'byung ba, khams] According to Indo-Tibetan Buddhist, medical, and astrological literature, these are the basic constituents of all material and phenomenal experience, and can be interpreted at various levels, ranging from that of coarse physical manifestation to the subtle aspects of the mental continuum. The four basic elements and their respective qualities are: earth (solidity), water (cohesion), fire (heat and transformation), and air (movement and energy). When five or six elements are enumerated, the additional ones are space and consciousness (or mind), respectively.

EJECTION OF CONSCIOUSNESS Also known as phowa (Tib. 'pho ba) [Skt. samkranti] The practice of ejecting or transferring the consciousness of the recently deceased to a pure realm such as Sukhavati. A qualified practitioner may perform the transference on himself, although the task is normally entrusted to a qualified lama.

EMANATION See NIRMANAKAYA.

FIVE WISDOMS (Skt. pancajnana) [Tib. ye shes lnga] Five types of fundamentally pure awareness which are ever-present within all sentient beings. These are normally obscured by karmic predispositions and bewilderment, and thus manifest as the five kleshas. The five wisdoms are: the wisdom of the expanse of reality, mirror-like wisdom, the wisdom of equanimity or sameness, the wisdom of discernment, and the wisdom of accomplishment. Each of the five is closely associated with one of the five buddha families.

FORTY-NINE-DAY PERIOD See INTERVAL.

GREAT LIBERATION THROUGH HEARING IN THE BARDO (Tib. bar do thos grol chen mo) Commonly known in the West as the Tibetan Book of the Dead. A treasure text of great importance composed in the eighth century by the acharya Padmasambhava of Oddiyana, and later discovered in the fourteenth century by the treasure revealer Karma Lingpa, it is a vast compendium of extensive and detailed knowledge and instruction pertaining to the interval.

GROUND CLEAR LIGHT See under CLEAR LIGHT.

GROUND CLEAR LIGHT INCREASE STAGE See APPEARANCE, INCREASE, AND ATTAINMENT.

GURU YOGA (Skt.) [Tib. bla ma'i rnal 'byor] A practice of devotion to the guru culminating in receiving his blessing and becoming inseparable with his mind. It is also the fourth preliminary practice of the Vajrayana ngondro.

ILLUSORY BODY (Skt. mayadeha) [Tib. sgyu lus] One of the six dharmas of Naropa, this advanced practice describes the experience of a practitioner who arises in a form resulting from the realization of the inseparability of the three kayas. This is predicated on authentic recognition of the illusory and dream-like nature of all phenomena, and is divided into two stages of attainment: impure and pure.

INCREASE STAGE See APPEARANCE, INCREASE, AND ATTAINMENT.

INTERVAL (Skt. antarabhava) [Tib. bar do] Generally, this term can refer to any of six different intermediate states of existence according to the Nyingma and Kagyu traditions. Most often, however, it specifically refers to the period between a being's death and subsequent rebirth, the duration of which is considered to last an average of about forty-nine days.

KLESHA (Skt.) [Tib. nyon mongs, dug] Emotional obscurations, afflicted emotions, or poisons. The three primary kleshas are attachment or desire, aversion or anger, and ignorance or bewilderment. Along with pride or arrogance, and envy or jealousy, they are collectively referred to as the five kleshas.

KÜNDZOP (Tib. kun rdzob, kun rdzob bden pa) [Skt. samvrtisatya] Often translated as "conventional truth" or "relative truth," the Tibetan literally reads "totally fake truth." This describes how ordinary sentient beings perceive the exitence of phenomena; it is considered to be true on a conventional level.

LIFE WIND (Tib. srog rlung) The subtle energy or "wind" that keeps the mind biologically seated in the physical body. The life wind abides within the avadhuti or central channel of the body.

LUMINOSITY See CLEAR LIGHT.

LUCID DREAMING See DREAM YOGA.

MENTAL BODY (Tib. yid lus) The form of subtle body experienced by an interval being, which is not confined to a gross physical form. See WIND-MIND.

MOTHER CLEAR LIGHT See under CLEAR LIGHT.

MOTHER LUMINOSITY See under CLEAR LIGHT.

NIRMANAKAYA (Skt.) [Tib. sprul pa'i sku] The body of emanation, through which buddhas manifest spontaneously and usually physically in accord with the diverse needs and dispositions of limitless sentient beings. The various possible types of emanation are classified in different ways according to either the Mahayana sutras or the perspective of the Vajrayana. In the specific context of this book, the third phase of the bardo is considered to be an ideal window of opportunity for an interval being to intentionally take rebirth as a nirmanakaya.

OM MANI PEME HUNG The common Tibetan pronunciation of the Sanskrit OM MANI PADME HUM, this is the well-known mantra of the mahabodhisattva of compassion, Avalokita (Skt.), or Chenrezik [Tib. spyan ras gzigs].

PATH CLEAR LIGHT See under CLEAR LIGHT.

PHOWA See EJECTION OF CONSCIOUSNESS.

RAINBOW BODY (Tib. 'ja' lus) A term referring to the experience of a highly accomplished tantric practitioner who entirely transcends the conventional limitations of physical form at the time of death, attaining a state of realization that in some cases may be equivalent to what is known as the body of great transference (Skt. mahasamkrantikaya) [Tib. 'pho ba chen po'i sku]. Outward evidence of such attainment may take the form of visible rainbows and the remaining presence of hair or fingernails following dissolution of the deceased's physical body.

RED ELEMENT The residual seed essence of the mother's ovum, obtained at conception, which remains present in the center of the body below the navel for the duration of a person's life.

SAMBHOGAKAYA (Skt.) [Tib. longs spyod rdzogs pa'i sku] The body of complete enjoyment through which buddhas appear perceptible only to bodhisattvas. Refers to the lucid, unimpeded manifestation of the mind's true nature, and within the interval experience this is primarily characterized by the appearance of the forty-two peaceful and fifty-eight wrathful deities. In this second phase of the interval, by transforming the appearance of your mental body into the body of the deity, you can achieve liberation in the sambhogakaya.

SINGED OFFERING (Tib. gsur) Burnt or singed offering. Consecrated herbs, barley, and other substances are singed and offered with an accompanying liturgy, which benefits beings in the bardo and otherwise.

SIX DHARMAS OF NAROPA (Tib. na ro chos drug) Naropa taught Marpa these tantric practices, which are an important part of the Kagyu teachings and a standard practice in the traditional three-year retreat. They consist of chandali (Tib. gtum mo), illusory body (Tib. sgyu lus), dream yoga (Tib. rmi lam), clear light (Tib. 'od gsal), interval practice (Tib. bar do), and ejection of consciousness (Tib. 'pho ba).

SIX ELEMENTS See under ELEMENTS.

THREEFOLD SHUTDOWN See APPEARANCE, INCREASE, AND ATTAINMENT.

TIBETAN BOOK OF THE DEAD See GREAT LIBERATION THROUGH HEARING IN THE BARDO.

VIDYADHARA (Skt.) [Tib. rig 'dzin pa]   Literally, "holder of awareness." An accomplished tantric master, especially one who purely holds the three vows—the pratimoksha, bodhisattva, and samaya. There are several particular classifications of vidyadharas. In the specific context of the bardo teachings, the vidyadharas manifest as powerful, dynamic beings embodying qualities of both the peaceful deities and the wrathful deities.

WHITE ELEMENT   The residual seed essence of the father's sperm, obtained at conception, which remains present in the center of the body at the very top of the head for the duration of a person's life.

WIND-MIND (Tib. rlung sems)   The mental body of an interval being, which is composed of the life wind and the all-basis consciousness or subtle mind.

YAKSHA (Skt.) [Tib. gnod sbyin]   One of four species that make up the lowest level of the desire god realms, often characterized with a menacing quality, bearing weapons.

YAMA (Skt.) [Tib. gshin rje]   Lord of Death, the personification of impermanence and the infallibility of cause and effect.

INDEX

absorption, meditative, 36, 39
aggregates, 66, 91, 102
  absence of, 29
  former, 52-53
agitation, experience of, 49-50, 52
alertness, 71-72
all-basis consciousness, 32, 43, 58, 102, 107
Amitabha, 82
  cycle of teachings, 77
  realm of, 76
anger
  and asura's pride, 63
  thirty-three forms "stop," 25
animal realm, 6, 64
animals, 47, 80, 97, 104
apertures, nine, 43, 76, 79
appearance, increase, and attainment, 24-29
appearances, 5-6, 11, 20
  absence of, 27
  of dharmata, 47
  dissolution stage of, 24-27
  and emptiness, 56
  interdependent, 9-10

transformation of, 58, 61
  of your body, 44-45
appearance stage, 24, 25, 26, 27, 29
Aspiration for the Bardo, 3
aspirations, 11, 90, 103
  achieve liberation, 19
  attain wisdom, 56
  buddha activity, 72
  conscious birth through, 109
  extreme simplicity, 38-39
  gaining certainty, 13-14
  maintain yogic practices, 68
  means of mantra, 58
  motivation of, 73, 96
  path of Vajrayana, 71
  remove bewilderment, 15
  remove obstacles, 57
  sambhogakaya, 59
  train in dream state, 55, 73
  true nature of bardo, 12
  trust in the teachings, 11
  undertake practices, 7
  when eating meat, 97
assistance, spiritual, 80-81
asura realm, 6

asuras, 47, 63
attachment, 63, 68, 110
attainment stage, 24, 27, 29,
    86, 106
augmentation. *See* increase
    stage
avadhuti, 31
aversion, 64, 110
awareness, cultivation of, 49-
    50, 56-57

bardo
    aspects of, 11-15, 19-21,
        23-29
    definition of, 6-7
    hunger and thirst in, 46
    nature of, 9-12
    three phases of, 7
bardo of the absolute or true
    nature, 11
bardo proper, 87
being dead, 19, 43-59
bewilderment, 13, 64, 72
    in the context of, 9-12
    in the dream state, 15, 69
    projections, 5-7
    seven forms "stop," 28
beyond limit, 11
bodhisattvas, 41
bodhisattva vow, 97-98, 103
body
    emanation, 20
    illusory, 19, 45, 69
    See also mental body
body of complete enjoyment, 19
body of great unity, 59
body, speech, and mind, 37-
    38, 75
Buddha, 5, 10-11, 76, 84
buddhahood, 37, 40, 97
buddha nature, 33
buddhas, 41
buddhas, names of, 26, 79-80,
    101
Buddha Shakyamuni, 109
Buddhists, 96, 101-2
Buxador, 39-40

categories of "two's," 11
    See also, dharmas, eight
        mundane
central channel, 31-32, 87
chandali, 69
Chatral Rinpoche, 40
Chenrezik, 82, 94-96
child clear light. *See under*
    clear light
child luminosity, 36
clear light, 20, 23, 27, 59, 69,
    93, 96-97, 108
    ground, 33-37, 41, 51, 86,
        88, 99, 107
    meditation on, 94
    mother (fundamental), 35-
        36
    path of, 19, 24
    path or child, 34-36, 86
cognition, 24-25, 27-28, 32
coma, 82-83
compassion, 41, 69, 72, 84
compassion and love, 20, 75,
    80, 90
conception, gestation, and
    birth, 72
conduct of extreme simplicity,
    38
consciousness
    all-basis, 32, 43, 58, 102,
        107
    of the deceased, 51
    ejection of, 27, 76-78, 83,
        92
    six main functions of, 28
consecration, 46
contemplation, 75, 93-94
corpse, 52-53, 62
craving, 67
culture, Tibetan, 93

Darjeeling, 25
days
    forty-nine, 44, 51, 80, 87-
        89
    three, 39, 87
    three-and-a-half days, 51

meditation, practice of, 20, 33-
35, 41, 75, 95
meditative state, 35-36, 38
mental body
of bardo beings, 45, 49-50,
66
identification with, 53
transforming appearance of,
57, 61, 89
merit, 70-71, 79
accumulation of, 75
dedication of, 73-74, 76,
98, 101-3, 112
Middle Way, 20, 34, 69
Milarepa, 37, 108-9
mind, vajra, 58
mindfulness, 71-72
mindlessness, 57
moral discipline, 70, 90
mother clear light. *See under*
clear light

Naropa, 108-9
natural rest, 111
near-death experience, 85-86,
105-6
nirmanakaya, 7, 87, 96, 98,
107
achievement of, 89-90
liberation in, 76
path of the, 19, 21
nirvana, 10-11
nonconceptuality, 35-36

obscurations, purification of,
75
obstacles, cultivating awareness, 56
offerings
butter lamps, 39
dedicated to the deceased,
98
of possessions, 54-55
singed, 46
OM MANI PEME HUNG, 82, 92,
94-96, 101, 104

Palpung Monastery, 40
parents, 26, 63-64, 91-92, 109
path of the clear light, 19, 24
path of the five wisdoms, 50
path of the illusory body, 19
path of the nirmanakaya, 19,
21
physical posture, 85
practice prioritization, 93
preta realm, 6
pretas, 47, 64-65, 67
projections, bewildered, 7, 13
pure realm, 70-72, 76, 79, 90
purification, 75

rebirth, 61, 76, 79, 87, 90, 98
approaching, 19-20, 89
in an artificial process, 106
avoiding negative, 68
five types of, 48, 50
four types of physical, 67-68
indication of type, 62-63
power of choice, 72
samsaric, 71
red element, 31-32, 43, 85-86
See also drops, seed
essences, white element
red light, 25-26
refuge, sources of, 5, 70
refugee camp, Tibetan, 39-40
religious traditions, 84-85,
101, 104
retreat master, 40
"returners," 99
ripening of karma, 90-91, 102

samadhi, 36, 39-40, 88
sambhogakaya, 19, 87, 96, 98
appearance of, 47-48
Kagyu presentation of, 89
liberation in, 20, 57-58, 61,
76
samsara, 5, 9-11, 13, 57, 103,
107
samsaric lights, 48-51, 90
sangha, 5

seed essences, 31-32, 43, 85, 107
  See also drops, red element, white element
"see the face of the bardo of the true nature," 12
self-blazing of bliss and warmth. *See* chandali
sense experiences, 14-15, 28, 45
sequence of dying, 24
singed offering, 46
six dharmas of Naropa, 55, 69
six elements of human realm, 71
six realms, 5-6, 47-48, 102-3
sleeping, 14, 73, 107
spiritual friend, 42
stages of dying. *See under* dying, process of
stillness of body, speech, and mind, 37-38
stupidity, seven forms "stop," 28
Sukhavati, 76
supercognition, 46
suppression of the thirty-three types of anger, 25

thoughts, types of, 25, 28
Thrangu Monastery, 40
threefold shutdown *See* appearance, increase, and attainment
threefold stillness, 37-38
Three Jewels, 54-55
three kayas, opportunities of, 88
three phases of the bardo, 7
three thieves of liberation, 56-57
Tibet, 39, 41, 93, 98, 100
Tibetan Book of the Dead, 81
truth
  absolute, 9, 11, 29
  relative, 12-13
tulku, 107

unconsciousness, 88
  dissolution process, 24, 66
  intervention, 26, 83
utter blackness, 27

vajra body, sound, mind, 58
Vajravarahi, 20
Vajrayana, practice of, 58, 71, 109
vegetarianism, 96-97
vidyadharas, 47
virtue, 79, 90-92, 103
visualizations, 6-7, 69, 82, 85, 108, 110-12

water element, 23
well-being, 35
white element, 31-32, 43, 85
  See also drops, red element, seed essences
white light, 24-25
will, living, 99
wind element, 24
wind-mind, 58, 102
wind of karma, 50-51
wisdom lights, five, 48-51, 89-90

yakshas, 65
Yamaraja, the Lord of the Dead, 66-67
yamas, 29

ACKNOWLEDGMENTS

We would like to express our appreciation and gratitude to Khenpo Karthar Rinpoche for giving us this clear and concise teaching on the bardo and for his blessings and guidance. We also wish to thank Lama Yeshe Gyamtso for his translating, Mary Young for transcribing the oral teaching, Sally Clay for editing, Julie Markle for the index, Jigme Nyima for the research, glossary, and copyedit, and Sharon Rosen for her proofreading. We thank Sandy Hu for her generosity and for getting this project going. We express our appreciation to KTC Hartford for organizing this teaching and to Vajra Echoes for the recording of Rinpoche's teaching. We have made our best effort to present Rinpoche's teachings as accurately as possible. However, if any parts are incorrect or unclear, we take full responsibility. We hope that, despite our shortcomings, all beings may benefit from these teachings.

Maureen McNicholas and Peter van Deurzen

Karma Triyana Dharmachakra

Karma Triyana Dharmachakra (KTD) is the North American seat of His Holiness the Gyalwa Karmapa, and under the spiritual guidance and protection of His Holiness Ogyen Trinley Dorje, the Seventeenth Gyalwa Karmapa, is devoted to the authentic representation of the Kagyu lineage of Tibetan Buddhism.

For information regarding KTD, including our current schedule, or for information regarding our affiliate centers, Karma Thegsum Choling (KTC), located both in the United States and internationally, contact us using the information below.

Karma Triyana Dharmachakra
335 Meads Mountain Road
Woodstock, NY 12498, USA
845 679 5906 ext. 10
www.kagyu.org
KTC Coordinator: 845 679 5701
ktc@kagyu.org

KTD Publications

GATHERING THE GARLANDS OF THE GURUS' PRECIOUS TEACHINGS

KTD Publications, a part of Karma Triyana Dharmachakra, is a not-for-profit publisher established with the purpose of facilitating the projects and activities manifesting from His Holiness's inspiration and blessings. We are dedicated to gathering the garlands of precious teachings and producing fine-quality books.

We invite you to join KTD Publications in facilitating the activities of His Holiness Karmapa and fulfilling the wishes of Khenpo Karthar Rinpoche and Bardor Tulku Rinpoche. If you would like to sponsor a book or make a donation to KTD Publications, please contact us using the information below. All contributions are tax-deductible.

KTD Publications
335 Meads Mountain Road
Woodstock, NY 12498, USA
Telephone: 845 679 5906 ext. 37
www.KTDPublications.org

THE BARDO PACKAGE

Through the auspices of Khenpo Karthar Rinpoche's tireless and compassionate efforts to benefit sentient beings, together with Dönden Chöjin Association, the Bardo Package has been created in order to help individuals prepare for the inevitable time of death.

The Bardo Package is an extremely rare collection of sacred items that have been produced with great care under the direct supervision and blessing of Khenpo Karthar Rinpoche. The importance of accuracy in the traditional rituals for the dying has been taken seriously, while at the same time being simplified to render the essential procedures easily accessible to anyone.

The Bardo Package will bring benefit when the moment of death requires immediate action, and will thus enable you to step forward and take control of the death situation without fear or confusion. If we can apply what we have learned in this life regarding dying, death, and the bardo, and also have the Bardo Package at our disposal, it will give us a greater opportunity for higher rebirth and liberation.

For further information:
www.dondenchojin.org
English (917) 880-8315
Chinese (516) 626-9285

Karma Chakme's Mountain Dharma as Taught by Khenpo Karthar Rinpoche, Volume One, translated by Yeshe Gyamtso and Chojor Radha, 2005

Karma Chakme's Mountain Dharma as Taught by Khenpo Karthar Rinpoche, Volume Two, translated by Yeshe Gyamtso, 2006

Precious Essence: The Inner Autobiography of Terchen Barway Dorje, Foreword by His Holiness the Seventeenth Karmapa, Ogyen Trinley Dorje, translated by Yeshe Gyamtso, 2005

The Vajra Garland & The Lotus Garden: Treasure Biographies of Padmakara and Vairochana, by Jamgön Kongtrul Lodrö Taye, Foreword by the Fourth Jamgön Kongtrul Rinpoche, Lodrö Chökyi Nyima, translated by Yeshe Gyamtso, 2005

Nyima Tashi: The Songs and Instructions of the First Traleg Kyabgön Rinpoche, Foreword by the Ninth Traleg Kyabgön Rinpoche, translated by Yeshe Gyamtso, English and Tibetan, 2006

Chariot of the Fortunate: The Life of the First Yongey Mingyur Dorje Rinpoche by Je Tukyi Dorje & Surmang Tendzin Rinpoche, Foreword by the Seventh Yongey Mingyur Dorje, translated by Yeshe Gyamtso, English and Tibetan, 2006

A Ceremony of Offering to the Gurus, Composed by the Glorious Gyalwang Karmapa Ogyen Trinley Dorje, translated by Yeshe Gyamtso; India 2006, USA, 2007

FORTHCOMING TITLES

Karma Chakme's Mountain Dharma as Taught by Khenpo Karthar Rinpoche, Volume Three, translated by Yeshe Gyamtso, Chojor Radha, Namgyal Khorko, 2007

Karma Chakme's Mountain Dharma as Taught by Khenpo Karthar Rinpoche, Volumes Four and Five, translated by Yeshe Gyamtso, 2008

Treasury of Eloquence: the Songs of Terchen Barway Dorje, translated by Yeshe Gyamtso, 2007

Garland of Jewels: the Eight Bodhisattvas, by Ju Mipham Rinpoche, translated by Yeshe Gyamtso, 2007

Tong-Len: Gentle Strength in Compassionate Living, by Lama Kathy Wesley, 2007